Women
Today

Women Today

TEN PROFILES

GRETA WALKER

HAWTHORN BOOKS, INC.
PUBLISHERS/*New York*

*For David
and for Naomi and Josh*

Contents

Women Today

Doctor, Lawyer, Conductor, Chief...

The women portrayed on these pages are not heroines of fifty years ago, nor are they superwomen doing fantastic deeds that no one could hope to emulate. They are hardworking, flesh and blood people, some famous, others little-known, who have fashioned meaningful careers for themselves in what used to be a man's world.

I have chosen to write about these particular ten women because they represent so many different backgrounds, interests, and goals. Some of the women are black, some white; a few are from poor backgrounds, others middle-class. Two suffered because they were Jewish and two felt like outcasts because they were bright; the black women experienced segregation in the south and deprivation of their civil rights. Many of the women married and raised (or are still raising) children while pursuing careers, and two chose to remain single and not have children. The women come from different parts of the country and experienced diverse culture patterns. One of the women, Marketa Kimbrell, came from Czechoslovakia, where she lived and suffered during the Nazi occupation. Lola Redford hails from the insular environment of Mormonism in Salt Lake City, Utah.

The reader will realize, after finishing this book, that there is no formula, no set pattern for constructing a life that includes a career. Each person must find her special way.

The one thing all the women in this volume have in common is that they found their most rewarding work when they followed their own instincts rather than conforming to some established pattern of behavior. By responding to their individual needs, they not only improved the quality of their own lives but brought change to the lives of other women as well.

Betty Friedan was trying to resolve her conflicts about her role as wife and mother when she wrote *The Feminine Mystique.* The book changed her life and the lives of thousands of other women as well. It also gave impetus to the beginning of the women's movement.

Eve Queler decided to become a conductor. In taking the hard road into the male-dominated world of conducting, she not only achieved satisfaction for herself but paved the way for other potential female conductors.

Marlene Sanders made similar inroads in television broadcasting, while Gertrude Schimmel helped open up civil service promotion for women in the New York City Police Department.

Dorothy Pitman Hughes needed a day care center for her preschool daughter. Finding that the rigid rules of city day care made her child ineligible, she set about to change the day care system in New York City and succeeded.

Gloria Steinem shed her social butterfly image in favor of a more rewarding feminist role. She helped found *Ms.* magazine, the most influential women's liberation publication in the country.

Each of the women in the book has had a similar impact by pursuing what was truly important and interesting to her.

Most of the women I have included are involved in the women's movement. Every thoughtful working woman is aware that there is an inequality of opportunity between men and women, with women usually getting the short end of the stick. Most women who are successful realize that the growing strength of the women's movement has made their struggle a little easier and can't help but lend it their support.

You, the readers, will eventually be embarking on careers of your own. It is likely some of you will choose to follow in the footsteps of women in this book. Others may elect careers in completely different fields. Whatever your choices, perhaps you will find more courage to make strong decisions and to accept your own inclinations, if you understand how these ten women followed the dictates of their concern and their instincts in shaping the quality of their lives.

Betty Friedan

In a basement room of an enormous, stark, futuristic apartment complex, Betty Friedan, author of *The Feminine Mystique* and the acknowledged instigator of the woman's movement, is teaching a class. She sits at the head of a long, plain table dressed in black pants and a print wraparound blouse. Her thick, silver hair is highlighted by the overhead fluorescent lights.

The men and women students, ranging in age from nineteen to seventy, sit around the table waiting expectantly for their instructor to discuss a paper that one of the women has just read.

The assignment Betty gave her class was to write a composition comparing the attitudes of people from different generations toward woman's role in society. When Betty read all the papers, she found that many of the students, especially the women, talked about themselves in their compositions, revealing their desires for better lives.

"I cried when I read these papers," Betty confided to a friend.

Now the woman who has just read her composition comparing her sixty-year-old self to her ninety-year-old mother waits nervously for her famous instructor to mete out criticism.

"The paper was wonderful," Betty says in her husky voice, and the woman smiles happily. The teacher goes on

to point out why she found the composition so excellent; she is impressed by the writer's analytic ability. She also advises the student as to where she might improve her writing skills.

Betty then turns to a black woman in her thirties and asks her to read what she has written. The woman says she doesn't want to, that she feels shy.

"Oh, you must!" Betty exclaims, impulsively reaching out her hand to the woman. "It's so good." The student is still reticent, but the enthusiastic instructor finally persuades her. As the woman reads, Betty listens attentively, smiling. Her eyes mist over, and her strong face, with its full mouth, heavy-lidded eyes, and slightly prominent nose, suddenly looks soft and lovely.

After all the papers have been read, Betty talks to her class about the necessity to restructure society as well as the need to achieve equality among the sexes. "We must change our institutions," she tells them. Although many of the students in the class are not highly educated, Betty addresses them as peers, reaching out to them, asking their thoughts and opinions, gesturing constantly with her expressive hands. It is obvious that she enjoys teaching this class.

A week later, in a fancier setting, Betty is a guest speaker at The Executive Woman dinner at New York's Biltmore Hotel. She is introduced as, among other things, cofounder of the new women's bank—a bank where women, for the first time, will hold major offices. Betty, dressed for the occasion in a long black gown, tells the assembled group of successful career women that she will talk about women and economic reality. Some of the realities she stresses are that women are still "the last hired and the first fired," that women must begin to understand the realities of power. "At this point women still can't run equally for office," she says. "We can't get money to run an adequate campaign." Her thesis is that men and women should share equally in the work load. "This would change the work structure, giving both men and women more freedom."

Unlike many spokeswomen for the women's movement, Betty Friedan does not see men as the enemy. "Men who work with women are not hostile," she tells her attentive audience. "The most hostile men are those who only deal with women in the context of the feminine mystique. Men and women must move together to restructure the society. We are not going to abolish the family. We are not going to abolish marriage. We are not going to abolish the office. But we can change the structure."

When the speech is finished, the assembled women applaud enthusiastically. Some of them have taken notes while she talked, while others simply listened raptly. The next day the newspapers will carry an item about the talk. When Betty Friedan speaks, it's an event to be reported.

It has not always been that way for this highly intelligent and innovative woman. Her growing-up years in Peoria, Illinois, were painful and full of rejection.

She was born Betty Naomi Goldstein in 1921, the oldest of three children. Her father, Harry Goldstein, owned a jewelry store, while her mother, Miriam, gave up her job as society editor of a local newspaper to assume the duties of wife and mother. Harry and Miriam had a tense relationship, and young Betty was constantly on edge, wondering when the next argument might erupt.

At school the brilliant, energetic, unconventional-looking young girl was an excellent student. She had a few girl friends, but her intense desire to be attractive to the boys met with no success. By the time she reached high school, even her handful of girl friends deserted her to join sororities that barred Jews. It was her first awareness of how minority groups suffer from injustice.

The lonely adolescent filled her life with writing poetry

and reading. Her father, fearful that his eldest daughter become too much of a bookworm, limited her library borrowing to five books at a time—a cruel punishment, she thought.

There were other compensations for her lack of social acceptance. She started a high school literary magazine, made the dramatic honor society, and became valedictorian of her 1938 graduating class. "I would have given them all up just to be popular," Betty says.

If high school in Peoria made her feel an outsider, Smith College and the east welcomed her intellect and gave her a sense of belonging. "It was a great, marvelous thing for me," Betty recalls. "An unfolding of the mind. And I wasn't a freak for it."

At Smith, Betty majored in psychology, wrote prize-winning editorials for *SCAN*, the college newspaper, and helped found the Smith literary magazine. She was at the top of her graduating class in 1942 and received her B.A. degree summa cum laude. She also earned the coveted Phi Beta Kappa key.

Still immersed in the field of psychology, Betty accepted a research fellowship at the University of California at Berkeley. At the end of a year she was offered a long-term fellowship that would involve studying for her doctorate. She turned down the fellowship because the young man she was involved with said to her, "You know I'll never be able to get such a fellowship. If you accept it, it will ruin our relationship."

Betty claims that her boyfriend's objections were only part of the reason for giving up the fellowship. "I had this sense," she remembers, "that I was going to be so much brighter than all the men, that if I stayed in the academic world I would be a spinster the rest of my life."

The romance came to an end despite the sacrifice, and Betty left California for New York. She shared a Greenwich

Village apartment with friends from Smith and began to do some writing for a news service and for labor newspapers.

Toward the end of 1946, Betty met blond, attractive Carl Friedan, at that time a summer-stock producer. Within two months Carl and Betty were sharing an apartment, and seven months later, in June 1947, they were married. It was a stormy marriage right from the start. Both the Friedans were volatile people and hardly a month went by without a fight erupting—very often a violent one—either in private or in public.

Betty's life began to change from that of a career woman to that of a housewife. Within eight years she and Carl had three children. The oldest, Daniel, was born in 1948, Jonathan in 1952, and Emily in 1956. In 1957 the Friedans purchased a large house in the suburbs. Betty Friedan was busy living what she would come to call "the feminine mystique" and hating it.

"Eight schizophrenic years of trying to be a kind of woman I wasn't," she later recalled to a magazine interviewer, "of too many lonesome, boring, wasted hours, too many unnecessary arguments, too many days spent with, but not really seeing, my lovely, exciting children, too much cocktail party chitchat with the same people, because they were the only people there."

Unlike most of her female neighbors, Betty continued to do some free-lance work—articles for women's magazines. "I was the only mother of my kids' friends who was doing work," she recalls. "I felt like a freak. I never talked about my writing. It was like my secret vice. I also didn't take my work terribly seriously."

In 1957 Smith College asked Betty to do a survey of her graduation class of 1942 for the fifteen-year reunion. The results would be read at the reunion dinner. Hoping to parlay the survey into a magazine article, Betty fashioned a questionnaire designed to find out how the women she had gone to school with were resolving the conflict between education and housewifery. The results were startling. Like Betty, her former classmates were dissatisfied with their limited roles as wives and mothers. Instead of answers, Betty received questions: "What do I do with my education?" "Is there nothing more to my life?" "Is this all?" asked many of the women.

Armed with these responses, Betty sat down to her typewriter. "I did an article for *McCall's*," Betty relates, "trying to show that women were not as happy as one might think in their homemakers' cocoons. The editor, who was a man, said women couldn't possibly feel the way I had portrayed them. He said he wouldn't print it. The *Ladies Home Journal* took it and then proceeded to rewrite it to conform to their image of the way things were. I wouldn't let them print it that way. I took it to *Redbook*, and the editor there said only their neurotic readers could identify with such a concept. I decided that the only way to present this information was to do a book."

Betty persuaded the unenthusiastic W. W. Norton publishing house to give her a $3,000 advance to write her untitled book about the dissatisfactions of women and their lack of equality in society.

"I expected the writing to take a year," Betty confides. "It took me five. Those were five lonely years. Even though I knew my idea was a good one, there were times when I'd ask myself, 'Am I crazy to think this way?' But I wasn't crazy. Even today, women come up to me and say, 'Your book changed my life.' "

W. W. Norton published *The Feminine Mystique* in 1963. They had no expectations that it would be successful and only printed 3,000 copies.

"But I knew I had something important," Betty recalls. "I also knew it had to be promoted."

She talked the reluctant publisher into hiring a free-lance

publicity woman to promote the book. Part of the campaign was to have the author appear on television talk shows. Inexperienced in this medium, Betty was not the perfect talk-show guest. She was so full of enthusiasm that she tended to speak too fast, and nobody could understand her. She also had a bad habit of leaving her sentences uncompleted. Still, *The Feminine Mystique* gained recognition despite its author's lack of polish on TV. Women all over the country responded to the theme of the book which stated that women were trying to live one way—as blissful housewives and mothers—while inside they felt deprived of being able to use their education and abilities.

The Feminine Mystique became an enormous success, selling over 60,000 hardbound copies and over 1,500,000 paperbacks. Letters from women throughout the country poured in daily telling the author that her book was relating their stories, that she understood what they were suffering.

As the book brought more and more success to Betty Friedan the author, it served to increase the unhappiness of Betty Friedan the wife. The Friedans had never been an idyllic couple, but as Betty became less the housewife and more the public figure, the strains between husband and wife mounted. There were frequent occasions for violence, and several times the famous author appeared on television talk shows sporting dark glasses to conceal a black eye.

In 1964 the Civil Rights Act was passed banning race and sex discrimination in employment, but it soon became clear that those in power were more interested in enforcing sanctions against racial discrimination than against discrimination in hiring practices toward women. A group of concerned women approached Betty and said, "You're the only one who can do it. You have to start an N.A.A.C.P. for women."

Betty was reticent. She had never been interested in women's groups and had always avoided them. Now she was being asked to start one. After some vacillation, she became convinced that this group would be totally different from the standard women's organization and agreed to participate. The National Organization for Women (NOW) was formed in 1966, and Betty was elected its first president.

As president of NOW, Betty Friedan the author-housewife became Betty Friedan the activist. NOW was established to achieve "full equality for women in America in a truly equal partnership with men." Its president went after that equality with a vengeance. She sent letters to President Johnson asking for legislation to help women elevate themselves to first-class citizenship. She sat in at the Oak Room of the Plaza Hotel in New York City during the lunch hour, a time reserved for men for the past sixty-one years. She and NOW protested ads that exploited women, came out against textbook publishers that devalued women in history, and refused to support political groups that wouldn't include women's rights in their platforms.

As her work for equal opportunities for women became more effective, Betty's marriage crumbled completely. The Friedans were divorced in 1969.

By 1970 NOW was a well-established organization with approximately 6,000 members in thirty-five chapters throughout the country. With its growth the organization began to see internal strife. Much of the opposition was directed against the president, Betty Friedan. Many of the women, some of them lesbians, wanted NOW to become more militant—more antiman. Betty disagreed. She didn't see men as the enemy and she was reluctant to blur the real issues—equal employment and equal pay—by raging impotently at men.

Faced with the unresolvable disagreements, she decided to step down from the presidency in 1970. For her final act as president she helped structure the August 26 Women's

Strike for Equality—"an instant revolution against sexual oppression"—to celebrate the fiftieth anniversary of women's suffrage. It was an awesome event. Thousands of women marched down New York's Fifth Avenue. Similar demonstrations occurred in other major cities across the country. The nation became aware that the women's liberation movement (as it had begun to be called) was something to be reckoned with.

Once she resigned as president of NOW, Betty had to reshape her life. She wanted to get back to writing, and, in fact, after the publication of *The Feminine Mystique* had signed a contract with Random House giving her a $10,000 advance to do another book. Her work with NOW had halted the project and she thought she might get back to it. But writing is a hard discipline requiring a great deal of solitary work. Betty was constantly in demand for lectures all over the United States and in other countries. It wasn't easy to confine herself to her desk and typewriter. There was also the problem of finances. Her expenses were high, and lecturing fees paid the bills.

In June 1971, in addition to her other activities, Betty started writing a column for *McCall's* magazine. "The bra-burning image," she wrote in her first column, "which enables people to dismiss us as a silly joke, can and must be replaced. That is why I have finally decided to do this column for *McCall's.*"

She used the space in the magazine to reveal many of her political and personal thoughts. She talked about her two boys going off to college and the adjustment she had to make in living with a much smaller family. In the August 1971 column Betty wrote, "It's the week of my fiftieth birthday, which I'm ashamed to admit I dread. I can't seem to come to terms with it." She told about a trip to London during that week, during which she met interesting people and was feted royally and during which she actually turned fifty and came to accept her new age. "I'm fifty on this magic day in the age of Aquarius. I'm my own age, and I feel glorious."

Early in 1971 Betty and other feminists began to talk about their desire to form a group that would serve to bring more women onto the political scene. The concept was fleshed out over five months of discussions, informal meetings, and long distance phone calls with women from various organizations in the country. Although the women had different political affiliations—some Democrats, some Republicans, and others not identified with any party— they all had a common concern about child care, abortion, welfare, and sex discrimination. In discussing the need for a politically oriented group, Betty observed in her September 1971 *McCall's* column, "It's a remnant of our own self-denigration, the put-down we finally do to ourselves, to think that a woman is 'pushy' or 'unfeminine' or on an 'ego trip' if she wants to run for political office. It is to be hoped that thousands of us are sufficiently liberated now to take on the necessary responsibility and demand the rewards."

The group became an actuality in July 1971 and was named The National Woman's Political Caucus.

In the spring of 1972 Betty was invited to Italy to make a series of speeches about the women's movement. Italy is a strong Catholic country, accustomed to male supremacy and female submissiveness, and Betty knew she might be going into unfriendly territory.

In Turin, a packed audience of women listened, fascinated, as Betty, through an interpreter, told them, "In America we have asserted the right to control our own bodies, we are demanding an approach to marriage and divorce that gives equal responsibility for home and children to husband and wife. Women in my country are no longer willing to do the menial work for half or none of men's pay, while men make all the decisions. We are even questioning sex discrimination in the church. Is God a he? Perhaps you will raise the possibility of a woman Pope. But I cannot say how it will happen." She received a standing ovation.

Things ran less smoothly in Milan. She spoke again to a vast audience of women, but this time Betty was given a male interpreter who distorted what she was saying. The women in the audience sensed the distortion and became furious. "That isn't what she's saying," they cried out. "We will not listen to a man," they screamed, and started converging on the stage. A woman interpreter was miraculously produced and peace was restored.

Throughout the next two years Betty continued to be a whirlwind of activity, lecturing, consulting, teaching, campaigning, and organizing. She covered both Democratic and Republican conventions in 1972 and afterward reflected in her *McCall's* column, "The women at both conventions were too inexperienced, too easily manipulated, too unsure of themselves to wield as much power as they might have."

She became involved in starting the first women's bank, and in November 1973 flew to San Francisco to address a meeting of the Bank Administration Institute. While there she hastily organized a news conference to express her dismay at President Nixon's involvement in the Watergate scandal and to urge women "to mobilize immediately" in a campaign urging Congress to move for impeachment of the president. "There is no way for us to be liberated," she said passionately, "if we lose our democracy."

Ever since her visit to Italy Betty had thought a great deal about the lack of power women have in the Catholic Church. Realizing that all changes must come from the top, she asked to have an audience with the Pope—not just to kiss his ring, she explained when she made her request, but to put forth her ideas about a need for a change in the Catholic hierarchy's attitude toward women. She was granted an audience early in 1974 with less than a week to prepare for it.

Wearing an elegant black dress and a small hat (she decided against a veil, since in the Jewish, Moslem, and Christian worlds the veiled head has always been the symbol of women's submission to an inferior status), she went to meet the Pope. Her gift for the Holy Father was a chain holding a gold-plated symbol of the women's movement.

The audience with His Holiness was brief, but Betty had time to say that she hoped "the Catholic Church would come to profound new terms with the personhood of women, and that when this happens the church and the Judeo-Christian tradition which have been a force holding women back for many centuries will become a force for the liberation of women."

The Pope told Betty that the church would really study the situation of women not only in the family but at work, in all the fields of society, so that women could develop according to their aspirations and play their proper roles.

"He took my hand in both of his," Betty wrote in her column, "as if he really meant his concern for women. He seemed much more human, somehow, than I had expected, with a warm and caring expression; he wasn't going through perfunctory motions in meeting with me; he seemed strangely intent, curious, interested in this meeting, which was going on much longer than anyone had given me reason to expect."

Betty Friedan lives on the fortieth floor of a large, modern, New York apartment house. One living-room window yields a breathtaking view of the Hudson River and the shores of New Jersey, while another offers a magnificent panorama of New York City.

The furnishings of the room reflect Betty's flair for the

dramatic. The Victorian chairs, couch, and settees are covered in bright fabrics—red and blue velvets and purple and pink prints. Oriental rugs cover the floor. One light fixture is of hammered metal from Mexico, and an Indian cloth covers a table.

Betty is up early on a crisp, fall morning, dressed in a red wool skirt edged with fringe, a matching weskit, and a black blouse. After drinking half a cup of coffee, she settles back on a royal blue velvet couch to talk about her future and how she envisions the future of the women's movement.

"I just hope I can finish everything I have to do," Betty begins with a sigh. "So many projects keep opening up that there is never enough time. Right now I'm teaching a course at Yale. I call my course The Sex Role Revolution—Stage II. It has all sorts of questions and missing links, but it's shaping up to a whole new set of puzzles, mysteries, problems, and hunches that go way beyond the woman question and the feminine mystique. I feel the same way about it as I felt when I was working on *The Feminine Mystique*. What I need is some time to very seriously follow my hunches into some libraries and into some delving and research. I'd like to put together another book the way I did my first one.

"The trouble is all the projects that come up are so good that I don't want to extricate myself from them," Betty says with a laugh. "They keep me more tied up in time than my children did when they were little. It's hard. Now I'm involved in the upcoming International Year of The Woman. The whole woman thing is moving all over the world, and it cuts across political systems. Other countries look to us for leadership because we're the only ones who have been doing it consciously for the past few years.

"As for the future of the women's movement, I think the breakthrough against sex discrimination has been made. That territory is all charted. That doesn't mean that there doesn't have to be militant fighting and lawsuits and so on to break through where the breakthrough hasn't happened. But now we have to go on to make basic changes in society. We need a different kind of home. We need a new structure of work hours, not just from the point of view of women, but the new woman also implies a new man. While women don't want to be isolated in these sexual ghettos where the home is the woman's domain and the workplace is the man's, in the same way the men have to say they don't want to be work instruments for the rest of their lives either.

"Maybe what's required now is that everyone have shorter hours of work—no overtime for anyone. There could be more flexibility in the sharing of jobs; one job could be held by two people, each working a different shift. We've got to get away from the usual sexism in the organization such as doctor and nurse or boss and secretary, with the higher positions always being filled by men. Maybe we even need a new approach to the very architecture of the home. These are some of the new things to think about.

"In terms of my personal future, I could see myself marrying again. I still like the idea of living closely with someone and being able to share delight and pain with one person within the framework of a sexual relationship. I think people who have that are very lucky. But it doesn't seem to be happening in many cases. I know a few couples who have become closer through the years, even as their children have grown up and left home. It works for them. For other people, perhaps changes occur. But I still think people need and are most happy with a long-term emotional commitment, whether it's sanctified by the state and the church in the name of marriage or whether it isn't.

"I rarely look back and think about what I might have done differently. It's such a fruitless exercise. I wasted a lot of years in unnecessary conflicts that both kept me from doing and making certain commitments to work that might have been satisfying earlier. Maybe I would have had more enjoyment from my children in early motherhood, although I did enjoy my children a lot. There are many positive values for me in those years. If I had the same ability to get it all together many years ago that I have now, I might have had a better life. On the other hand, I might not have had the conflicts that led me to write *The Feminine Mystique.*" Betty shrugs philosophically. "So who can say?"

Dorothy Pittman Hughes

Happy birthday to you,
Happy birthday to you,
Happy birthday, dear Dorothy,
Happy birthday to you.

The plump, beautiful black woman finishes her gospel rendition of the time-worn song and the room full of black and white people applaud vigorously. The guest of honor, a stunning six-foot figure in white crepe halter top pajamas and high heeled shoes, rises to acknowledge the applause.

She is Dorothy Pitman Hughes and her birthday party is being held in a large, very long, shabby, one-room office. The colored lights, crepe paper decorations, and the music of the three-piece band give the room, with its file cabinets pushed against the wall, the atmosphere of a discotheque.

Grinning broadly, Dorothy blows out the candles on her birthday cake and sits down to listen to the speeches in praise of her. Clearly she is somebody special to the people present. They extol the work she has done in the west side New York community and speak lovingly of her as a human being.

When the speeches are finished, Dorothy's eight-year-old daughter, Patrice, starts to sing in a sweet, naturally musical voice. Dorothy beams and her whole body rocks

with the child's song. "Oh, sing it, daughter," she cries out several times. But Patrice has forgotten the ending of the song and begins to cry. Dorothy rushes to her and bending down, envelops the tearful child in her arms. "Don't cry, daughter," she urges in a soft southern voice. "I never can remember the end of the song when I sing."

Later, the guests leave the party and go out onto the ugly west side New York street with its graffitied walls, run-down brownstones, and dilapidated hotels. As they walk west, they must pass an impressive four-story modern building painted bright blue and red with a transparent yellow column running the length of the structure—a startling contrast to the drabness of the block. On the face of the building are printed the words "WEST 80th STREET COMMUNITY CHILD DAY CARE CENTER."

The guests know that visitors come from all over the world to examine the architecture of this structure and to observe the work going on inside. They also know that thirty families (many of whom were present at the party they have just left) fought for five years to get this building and to maintain within its walls a day care center that would be governed not by some uninterested board of directors but by the parents of the children themselves.

Above all, they are keenly aware that the struggle, with its exhausting years of fund-raising, meetings, sit-ins, demonstrations, and frustrations for this parent-controlled day care center, owes most of its success to the formidable, uncompromising leadership of the woman who has just celebrated her birthday.

She was born Dorothy Ridley on October 2, 1938, in the small town of Lumpkin, Georgia—population approximately 2,500—the third of ten children (eight of whom survived). Her father worked in the town's lumber mill, and her mother did domestic work as well as pick peanuts and cotton.

Dorothy's mother was a strong woman with a fierce streak of independence and great pride in her blackness. "My father was more mild," recalls Dorothy. "My father was the sort of person who did not rock the boat at all. My mother not only rocked it, she always shook it for anything that had to do with her life and her being free. And yet, I understand my father's position and I love him for staying alive. In those days an outspoken black man didn't live very long."

When she was ten, Dorothy started working after school as a domestic. She would knock on doors and ask the white families if they could use her. Often, if she wasn't needed, the door would simply be shut in her face.

Her mother took her to the peanut and cotton fields, but Dorothy couldn't work in them. The smell nauseated her and she immediately threw up. Today she feels she threw up because she thought the work was humiliating.

The all-black school that Dorothy attended was in an old building on the verge of collapse. She hated the education, which taught her white history and never mentioned anything about blacks.

To show her disapproval of the teaching, Dorothy would disrupt the class by singing hymns and encouraging all the other kids to join in. Other times she would come to class with a book by the black author James Baldwin. "When the teacher threw the textbook stuff at us," she recounts, "I'd come back with quotations from James Baldwin, and the other students would pick up on it. We ended up having rap sessions on racism."

While in high school, Dorothy decided she would go north after graduation and become a "fantastic, great singer." She had been performing at the nearby army base,

Fort Benning, and she was sure she was destined for star-dom.

The easiest way for a young black girl to go north was as a domestic. In 1956, when she was eighteen, an employment agency got Dorothy a job with a white family in Malverne, Long Island, a middle-class suburb of New York City. Her salary was twenty-eight dollars a week.

She was terribly excited. She had been hearing for years that New York was a melting pot—just one big family regardless of race, color, or creed. "So," she recalls, "when I came here, I decided I was going to melt."

The job lasted four months. Dorothy quit because the family she worked for insisted she walk the family dog. Her feeling was that if they wanted a dog, they should walk it themselves. She took her own apartment in the suburbs and did domestic work by the day. At night she sang in local bars.

All the while, she was becoming aware that equality in the north was a myth. The racism and classism were not as out in the open as in the south but were there just the same. Toward the end of 1957 she moved to Manhattan and started to look about for ways to change things.

She talked to the men she dated about the struggle of the black in America. "They all thought I was nuts," says Dorothy. "That was a period when all the black men were trying to be like white folks. They didn't want to hear about any struggle. I can't say that I had arrived at the point of being a whole person. I was still dressing the way I thought men wanted me to dress. Yet I knew something was terribly wrong."

Through her nineteenth and twentieth years, Dorothy often worked as a domestic during the day and as a disc jockey in a bar at night and tried to break in as a singer. During one harrowing period she was averaging two and a half hours of sleep a night. She wanted to make it on her own and not ever have to depend on her family.

And then, when she was twenty-one, Dorothy became pregnant after having her first sexual experience. When she recovered from her initial shock, she made two decisions: to have the baby and not to marry the father. "I didn't see any reason," she says, "to marry a man that I didn't want to share the rest of my life with. I decided against an abortion because I had too much respect for life. Besides, abortions were illegal then and there was no guarantee that one would be performed without physical danger to me. I'm awfully glad today that I made that decision."

Her daughter, Delethia, was born on February 10, 1960. Her birth forced twenty-two-year-old Dorothy to reevaluate the kind of life she wanted for herself and her child. "I could see that being a black woman singer was hard," relates Dorothy. "I realized I couldn't do the things that meant success."

A year and a half after Delethia was born, Dorothy met Bill Pitman, a feisty, dark-haired Irishman who had been in the Irish Republican Army. Here, at last, was a man who would talk to her about the inequities in the system and the struggle to overcome them. Like Dorothy, he had come to New York looking for the melting pot that had been depicted in the American movies he had seen back in his homeland. Like Dorothy, he had been disappointed. They saw the struggle in Ireland as a parallel to the black struggle in America. They were revolutionary allies. Dorothy dates the beginning of her serious political life to the day she met Bill. They were married in 1962 and took an apartment on West Eightieth Street. Their daughter, Patrice (named after the assassinated Congolese leader, Patrice Lumumba), was born March 10, 1965.

The 1960s saw the emergence of a strong civil rights

movement with which the Pitmans became involved. Among other things, they helped raise money for the first march on Washington in 1963 and participated in a pilgrimage to Harper's Ferry to honor the memory of the southern abolitionist John Brown. Deciding that they could do the most good at home, they started to work for decent housing within the West Side community.

To document landlord neglect of poor peoples' homes, Dorothy and Bill would climb the rickety stairs of rat-infested, heatless tenements and brownstones. Dorothy recalls barking dogs being set upon them by irate superintendents, and in 1964, when she was pregnant with Patrice, she had the frightening and dangerous experience of being pushed down a flight of stairs by an angry landlord.

During this period of intense political activity, Dorothy decided it would be helpful if she could leave her four-year-old daughter, Delethia, in a city day care center while she was out working. When she made inquiries, she found out that only very poor people could use the city day care centers, and then only after they had gone through the humiliation of proving their poverty. Recalls Dorothy, "I was horrified to find that these poor women had to dress in ragged clothes and say their husbands left or beat them before they could have their children accepted. Then, when they did get their kids in, nobody bothered to teach them anything. Day care centers were just places to leave a child for eight hours or more. To top it off, parents had no say in how the centers were run."

Another stipulation that enraged her was that children had to be over three years old. "I saw children under three in my neighborhood," says Dorothy indignantly, "who weren't being taken care of properly while their parents were at work. That's when I got interested in starting a different kind of day care center—one without all the qualifying restrictions."

Dorothy rang doorbells in her neighborhood to find out if others shared her interest. When people said they did, she invited them to a meeting. Only one woman came. Undiscouraged, the two women drew up a flier announcing another meeting and distributed it in the neighborhood. At the next meeting thirty families were represented. They became the West 80th Street Committee (because most of them lived on that street) and began their five-year struggle to build a center and to own their own building.

The group allied itself with the all-white, middle-class West 80th Street Block Association. They formed a day care committee with Dorothy as chairperson. However, it soon became evident that the block association didn't really want a day care center in the neighborhood. "It made them nervous," remembers Dorothy, "to think of a lot of black, poor children mixed in with their middle-income, white children. They kept trying to discourage us."

Bored with talking, the Pitmans drew up a proposal stating their aims: a parent-run center; parents as board of directors; children of all preschool ages admitted, including infants; people of all incomes admitted; talented teachers would be hired, even if they didn't have college degrees. Then they and the other families cleaned up the storefront office (with a kitchen in back) that they had been using for housing work and started taking in children from 7:30 A.M. to 7:30 P.M. Parents who didn't work cooked, took care of the children, and rounded up toys and educational equipment.

At the end of a month they were caring for forty-five children, including babies as young as nine months, and charging five dollars a week to those who could afford it to pay for rent and food. There were children of all colors and economic backgrounds. Here was the melting pot the Pitmans had dreamed of.

Through the first year there were no salaries for anyone.

The exception was one week when after paying for supplies they were left with nine dollars. Dorothy distributed the money equally among the forty-five workers, and each one received twenty-one cents.

One day the storefront was visited by two women—one from the health department and one a city day care representative. They wanted to close the center because it didn't have a city license and was illegal and because there were building violations. Furious, Dorothy lashed out at them, "Yes, we have violations, but you should see the homes some of these children live in. Many are on the fifth floor and they're real firetraps. Here we're on the first floor and we have enough adults to look after the children."

Although she was able to persuade the women to leave them alone, it was becoming apparent that being left alone was not enough. They needed money from the city to survive. However, when they went to the city, they were denied funds because they wouldn't conform to city restrictions.

In the summer of 1967 the federal government's Office of Economic Opportunity (OEO) gave the group $10,000 for a summer day care program to be run in one of the city schools. But instead of Dorothy and the thirty other families being in charge, a group from the block association gained control. "I was really mad," recalls Dorothy. "I knew these people would run it just like a city day care center. I decided I wouldn't work with them, even if the other families did."

The summer was not successful, and in September the funding was dropped. The parents came to Dorothy in a panic asking, "What are we going to do?"

"First," she told them, "I want a letter from you saying I have your full support. You also must be willing to serve as board of directors as we originally planned." The parents signed the letter.

Then all thirty families, with thirty-five children in tow, went to the local OEO ofice. They joined the dozens of other people waiting in the rain who, like themselves, were hoping to get funds. When the people inside saw the children getting drenched, they immediately took Dorothy and her group first. Whether it was to get rid of all the dripping kids in their office or because they realized that Dorothy's ideas were different from the summer program, the OEO people granted them $72,000 for a year's funding, with the provision that each month Dorothy would come and prove that the center was truly worthy of the money.

The funding enabled Dorothy, as director, to get a salary of thirty dollars a week and for the center to rent larger space on the ground floor of the Endicott, an old run-down hotel around the corner from the storefront. The Endicott housed winos, prostitutes, and addicts, and the owner of the hotel did as little as possible for his tenants. The day care center was continually plagued with roaches and insufficient heat. Worst of all, one day the ceiling fell in. Luckily, no one was hurt.

Through all this, the parents kept an attractive environment for the children. The gaily painted rooms were equipped with donated toys and educational materials, and the smell of healthy food emanated from the kitchen. Dedicated teachers were hired, including some who were untrained but very talented. In fact, eventually funding included an unprecedented concession—money for teachers to get further training while working at the center.

Still, they knew they must get out of the Endicott. Dorothy began to look around for a building they might buy. "I felt," she says, "that poor people, who had never owned anything, needed ownership of something before they could move their lives." When she saw the building on West Eightieth Street, it housed a Chinese restaurant and a dance hall, but it had a lot of space, and once renovated, would be perfect for their needs. Now there was a new struggle: raising money to buy a building.

Dorothy had not let up on her attempt to get city funds. They especially needed city money now in order to guarantee the bank that they would be able to meet mortgage payments on the building. Then the families made a discovery. "We found out," says Dorothy, "that the city had $8,000,000 in a day care budget that they were not using. We said to ourselves, 'Why should we take antipoverty money that could go to other causes when there's city day care money not being used?' So we started putting pressure on the city."

One effective form of pressure was the sit-in. There were many varieties, but the following is fairly typical: Dorothy would make an appointment at the Department of Social Services. Then she would show up with thirty families, thirty-five children, and some friends and neighbors. The strategy was to keep the employees from working. The adult demonstrators would talk to the workers about their problems or would march around the room clanking garbage-can covers and chanting. The children took over the telephone or scribbled pictures on the demeaning day care application forms.

The sit-ins brought them attention and some sympathetic reporting from the newspapers. Many local and national politicians became interested in their struggle. Gloria Steinem wrote several articles about them (she and Dorothy became close friends and later toured the country together, speaking for the women's movement). James Brown hosted a fund-raising party, as did other famous people, and the internationally renowned violinist Isaac Stern gave a benefit performance for them.

Through all this, Dorothy's life had taken on the aspect of a merry-go-round. She would work in the center during the day, meet with city officials several times a week, organize and participate in demonstrations (at least four a month), go to meetings in the evening, and try to fulfill her role as wife and mother. She was always available to people in the community who came to her for help.

Bob Gangi, head of the Action Corps, a group of Robert Kennedy's supporters who helped raise money for the day care center building, remembered, "Her house was like Grand Central Station. People were always running in and out. It drove me crazy. I could never talk to her alone."

Gangi also recalls that through the most hopeless periods, Dorothy inspired everyone. "She wouldn't quit and she wouldn't compromise," he says with admiration. "In addition, she was charming, beautiful, and intelligent," He conjures up an image of a handsome, long-legged, mini-skirted woman sailing into a meeting a half hour late, disarming everyone with a demure smile and a bit of southern accent, "Aren't I just awful to be so late?" and then astounding the assemblage with her political knowledge and intellect. "By the end of each meeting," remembers Gangi, "Dorothy had everyone saying yes to anything she wanted. I'm certain if she hadn't come to those meetings, community-control day care would have been defeated."

Aware of the strength she had accumulated, Dorothy did something unusual. She bypassed all the underlings and red tape and went directly to the commissioner of Social Services. She demanded city funding with no strings attached. He couldn't turn her away. By then she had too much political support.

The first city funding came through in the fall of 1968, but, as with the OEO money, they had to renegotiate every three months, which kept them in a state of anxiety. Dorothy's salary went up to $125.00 a week.

The year 1968 also saw the end of the Pitmans' marriage. Dorothy had felt for some time that the marriage was based solely on shared political interests, but hadn't acted on her feelings until she met Clarence Hughes, a warm, intelligent, politically concerned black man, and fell in love with him. On September 27, 1969, Dorothy Pitman became Dorothy Pitman Hughes. Dorothy and Bill have remained good friends.

Toward the end of 1969, the dream of owning their own building became a reality for the thirty families. With the aid of two mortgages, some loans, and private fund-raising, they had come up with the incredible sum of $500,000.

The renovation of the building took two years. It was completely gutted and then redesigned exactly as the parents wanted it.

As they waited to move into their new quarters, the Endicott became even more unendurable. As Dorothy says, "When you know things can be beautiful, it's oppressive to live in conditions that are not beautiful."

In September 1971 a party was given to celebrate the opening of the new building. Welfare families, celebrities, and city officials drank toasts together in honor of the event. A radiant, smiling Dorothy moved among the guests. She was filled with many emotions—a sense of great victory, a feeling of relief that part of the fight was over, and the sad knowledge that there would be more struggle to come. She was right. Three weeks later the city told them they would no longer be funded. A day after the notification, Mayor John V. Lindsay, who was seeking the Democratic nomination for president, found his campaign headquarters occupied by angry mothers and children accompanied by sympathetic reporters. The program was funded.

As director of the new building, Dorothy's salary went up to $200.00 a week. She was also made president of the West Side Alliance, which was set up, among other things, to assume ownership of the building. In time, being both landlord and director began to create conflicts within her. Then there were her children, who needed her attention (in February of 1971, Dorothy gave birth to a third daughter, Angela, named after the black revolutionary woman Angela Davis). She recalls walking down the street and suddenly feeling frightened by all the people who were dependent on her.

She also had a sense that some of the parents were abdicating their own responsibility, and when something came up they would say, "Oh that's no problem, Dorothy can handle it." Many of the parents, in turn, asserted that they wanted more control but that Dorothy insisted on doing everything herself. Some said it was hard for her to ask for help.

As the political climate became more conservative in the 1970s, the West 80th Street Day Care Center found it increasingly difficult to hold out against the demand of the city that they conform to their rules. They were now being forced to question applicants' incomes, and restrictions on the hiring of teachers were being imposed on them. Dorothy began to feel that if day care, which is tied up with welfare, was to have any permanent change, the welfare system would have to be radically altered.

She decided to direct her considerable energies toward affecting that change, and in January 1973, she resigned as director. Three weeks before leaving, she managed to have her salary raised to $16,350 a year—the highest salary for any day care director in the city. She could also point with pride to the fact that there were now over 100 community-controlled day care centers in New York State. When she had started in day care, there were none.

Eight o'clock on a warm summer night. Dorothy, Clarence, and the two older girls have finished the supper dishes. Delethia, a tall, graceful thirteen-year-old with a short Afro, and Patrice, a pixieish, long-haired eight-year-old, go upstairs to do their homework. Two-year-old Angela, a tiny replica of Dorothy, plays with objects on the large coffee table while Dorothy and Clarence rest for a moment. They look with pride at the golden oak paneling around the fireplace and windows that they stripped down themselves and at the exotic brown and white wallpaper, which was a do-it-yourself project also. In fact, the whole house has been lovingly worked on by its owners.

The Hugheses, both advocates of ownership, bought the three-storied house in 1972. That their home is situated on an unattractive street in Harlem, New York's black and Puerto Rican ghetto, doesn't bother them. The house is beautiful, the price was right, and they have hopes the neighborhood will improve.

Clarence goes upstairs to put Angela to bed, and Dorothy settles back to talk with a visitor about her feelings as a day care director, a feminist, and a wife and mother.

"In retrospect, I realize if you're the organizer of something, it's not wise to be the director, too. You don't stay detached enough. When the staff was sort of falling down in their work, I couldn't say, 'Hey, you've got to work harder,' when I understood why they couldn't. After all, we struggled for so many years. People can't keep all the zeal and energy for such a long time. If I hadn't been the director and been working so hard as I was, I would have been more relaxed during the low energy periods. Instead, I would get irritated and yet I couldn't push at people.

"Before I left as director, I began to feel that psychologically I was around a bunch of dead people—dead about helping anyone else. Now we were ninety families, and when we started we were thirty. Our first thirty families were able to build a whole building. I thought ninety families should be able to do something for ninety other families if we were moving with the same spirit. I never saw day care as only a way of freeing parents to look out for themselves. I saw it as a way of freeing children and parents together so they could relate to each other more.

"My kids think they would like me to be the mother who stays home, but that's because they don't know anything about that mother. That mother doesn't have her own life, so she has to dominate the kids and not let them have their freedom. I tell my children that I'm always available to them for anything they need me for, because I think any- one, even adults at times, would like other people to make decisions for them. I'm comfortable with decisions and eventually I want my children to feel the same way.

"Delethia idolizes me too much. She'd really like to be just like me. I keep saying to her, 'Be yourself.' I want them all to develop themselves in their own way. Of course, I do know that they can't help but be influenced by what I believe in. For example, I'm very active as a feminist, and my kids are very conscious of women's rights.

"The women's movement is very natural for me. The rap sessions, which were new to a lot of the sisters, were part of my growing up. My family and their friends would congre- gate on some person's porch each night and talk about the problems of living with their husbands and bringing up their children. They talked about sexism and racism, and we kids were usually around listening.

"We try to talk things out in our family today. If there's a conflict between my husband and me, we don't go to sleep until it's dealt with. If the children fight, I tell them, 'Don't go to bed in anger.' Maybe my attitude comes from my old religious beliefs that you don't have control over how long your life will be and you shouldn't destroy it by using it in anger.

"When I get angry, it's usually not at a person. I always respect people for their humanness, but I don't always respect their ideas. So I'm usually angry at an idea. I'm not a grudge-carrier. When I'm bothered by something, I have to let it out, and people can accept it or not."

Shortly after resigning as director, Dorothy was back on West Eightieth street in a storefront, ready to start the struggle to alter the welfare system. At this writing, she and a small group of people are having endless meetings about their project and the possibilities of getting funding. Heartened by $10,000 from the Whitney Foundation, they are looking to other funding groups and trying to solidify their own plan of attack. They are not sure yet what their strategy will be, but whatever it is, if Dorothy is involved it will have an impact.

Between meetings Dorothy makes telephone calls or dashes about getting city funding for a day care center in the Bronx, meeting with city officials about money for a new paint job for the West 80th Street Day Care Center, taping a black feminist television show, and taking her children to and from school (Angela is at the day care center).

"I'm not alive," says Dorothy, as she rushes from one appointment to another, "unless I'm fighting abuse and injustice. Those people who don't fight back are dead."

Marketa Kimbrell

In the auditorium of the Bronx Prison, Marketa Kimbrell, dressed in blue pants and a work shirt, sat on the floor surrounded by twenty attentive inmates. She was fatigued, and her large-featured face, devoid of makeup, looked haggard. She had been up the night before working on a script for her street theater ensemble, and after little sleep, she was conducting her weekly theater workshop at the prison.

A week later at 9:30 in the morning, Marketa's theater group is bringing a show to the same prison. The actors have hung hand-painted curtains, home-made posters and crepe paper in the drab room. Their stage is a high platform with another acting area below. Aretha Franklin's voice sings out on their tape recorder.

The inmates assemble by 10:00 A.M. and sit waiting for the show to begin, clapping their hands to the singing of Aretha.

In her slightly European accented voice Marketa announces the show, *The Mother*, explaining the plot: Upon the platform will be enacted Christ's three stages of the cross; the players on the upper stage will wear masks; below will be enacted the travails of a modern soldier deserting an unnamed war.

The inmates are attentive throughout the performance, laughing sometimes inappropriately but responding with anger when characters in the play try to muzzle the soldier from speaking out against the war and cheering when the mother and her friends are able to outwit those who would keep them quiet.

After the performance an inmate who is part of her workshop talks to Marketa about his imminent release and his desire to join her company.

The warden congratulates her on the show, saying that he doesn't agree with her message but he respects her right to say it.

The men crowd around her, shaking her hand, talking, loathe to leave. In the play Marketa had portrayed a strong peasantlike middle-aged woman. Now standing among the crowd of men, she resembles a young girl.

Marketa Kimbrell is one of those extraordinary women who, with absolutely no artifice, can look radiant, and she is especially beautiful when she is doing the work she cares about intensely—bringing theater to the poor and forgotten.

To this end, she conducts prison workshops and operates a street theater group. Her ensemble performs in prisons during the winter and in poverty areas throughout the country in the summer.

To support herself, her elderly mother, and two of her three sons (one is out on his own), she teaches acting classes for film directing students at New York University. Her class is one of the most popular in the department.

Marketa's company is composed of black, white, and Hispanic women and men in their twenties. Some are from great wealth, others are ex-inmates or ex-addicts. Marketa has great respect for her actors' ideas and will often defer to them, but she does make demands. Actors must work long hours, give the best they have, and use no drugs around the theater. Although she, personally, is against even marijuana, her antidrug attitude is more cautious than moral.

"Our plays are political," explains Marketa, "and in many places we perform the police would love to find an excuse to stop us. I've worked too hard to have everything go down the drain because someone can't do without grass."

Some of the young people in Marketa's acting class are eager to join her company, but she will take only the truly committed. The tours are physically exhausting, as the actors travel by truck, often over rutted, hardly used roads. Frequently they live with the families they perform for, sharing their harsh way of life.

Marketa is no stranger to hardship. She has lived through many difficulties and has survived a harrowing period of history.

Marketa Kimbrell was born in Czechoslovakia in August 1928. Her family name was Naičova. Her father, an imperial forester, cared for the woods outside Prague which belonged to a very wealthy Jewish family. The Naičova family had been foresters for generations. Marketa's paternal grandparents were Austrian aristocrats, and she recalls her father's preoccupation with the ways and looks of the aristocrats. When she was young, he urged her to sleep on her nose because he thought it was beginning to resemble the maternal Czechoslovakian nose, which he considered unaristocratic.

Marketa, an active, independent girl, was her father's favorite over her two brothers and sister. He would bring home injured animals for her to care for, and she remembers deer living in her house and guinea pigs that she pushed in a doll's carriage. So deep was her attachment to the animals that when hunters would come in with a deer, she'd throw herself hysterically over the dead animal.

In 1938 the Germans occupied Czechoslovakia. When the forests were confiscated by the Nazis, Marketa's father lost his job. Hoping to find employment, the family moved to Prague. Then Marketa went to the gymnasium (a sort of combination high school and junior college), where she took courses toward a career as an airplane pilot. When the Germans decreed that girls should take only domestic classes, Marketa cut her long pig-tailed hair and led the other students in a revolt. She was dismissed from the school, signaling an end to her formal education.

Her mother wanted Marketa to take an office job to help out the family finances, since her father was still jobless. Passing by the State Theatre one day, Marketa decided that being an actress would be better than working in an office. And besides, she had always loved opera and theater. She appeared at the stage door declaring that she was there to become a member of the company and that she knew the entire role of Donna Anna from Mozart's *Don Giovanni*. Impressed, the directors asked her to do an aria for them. What she had failed to tell them was that she couldn't sing at all and knew only the words. Her audition consisted of saying the repetitive phrases of the aria with gestures but without music. The directors roared with laughter, but something in this gawky girl must have caught their fancy. They gave her two audition pieces to work on at home, and when she returned and performed them, they accepted her into the company and gave her a scholarship.

Marketa's life became the theater. During her apprenticeship she studied voice, dance, and acting. She started with small parts, gradually was given more important roles, and finally, when a leading actress became ill and couldn't go on in a play, the director coached her for three days and she went on to brilliant reviews that hailed her as a new star.

Her joy was short-lived. Soon the Nazis closed the theater and took all the company into work camps. From 6:00 A.M. to 6:00 P.M., Marketa worked in a cable factory where the conditions were so severe that she contracted a lung disease and was sent to the hospital. The day she checked out of the factory in May 1945, American planes bombed it, killing everyone inside. It was the last gasp of the war. Prague was being bombed and fires were raging everywhere. Frightened and desperate, Marketa and her sister Marta, along with some other refugees, stole a car and headed for the Czech border. There were many cars on the road and the going was slow. As they approached the border, a bomb fell, demolishing the automobile in front of them. Marketa and her friends jumped out of their car and hid in the bushes. A minute later their car went up in flames.

"My childhood," recalls Marketa, "was running from bombs, seeing friends hit, and helping dig people out from under buildings."

Marketa and Marta were picked up by the Russians and given the choice of a Russian or an American prison camp. They chose the American camp because they figured the food would be better. From the prison camp they were sent to a displaced persons camp. The seventeen-year-old Marketa was granted permission to read the daily news over the loudspeaker. After a while she added a poem at the end of the news report. Her news and poems became so popular that people urged her to help them perform skits. By the time she and her sister were discharged in 1947, they were doing full-length plays.

From Heidelberg, where they were released, the sisters went to Paris, where Marketa was offered a job as a singer with an American black band. The musicians taught her American songs phonetically, and although she recalls that she was terrible, she does remember being fairly good as a Marlene Dietrich imitator.

"I was paid in food stamps, so I did have enough to eat. But I had no money to buy clothes. My clothes were a pair of character ballet shoes, an old pair of boy's slacks, a tattered skirt made out of an Italian curtain, and a Bavarian coat I'd found in the DP camp. I had fancy costumes to sing in, so I looked pretty good on stage. Often a man would ask to take me home after the show. Then I'd appear in my shabby clothes, and you could see the poor man's face fall with disappointment."

While in France, Marketa saw a Red Cross newspaper with a picture of her and her sister and the news that her parents felt the two girls were dead and were asking for information about them. Since both sons had been killed, it meant that her parents assumed they had lost all their children.

She decided to go past the Iron Curtain into Czechoslovakia and find her parents. It was ten days till Christmas. Marketa was determined to arrive on Christmas Day. With no money and as much food as she could carry, she started hitchhiking to Prague. Most rides came from American and Russian army trucks, but there were sometimes hours between rides, and the cold was penetrating. Her best lift was from the engineer of a coal train. He let her ride with him in the engine cab, where it was marvelously warm, and even shared his lunch with her.

True to her resolve, Marketa arrived in time for Christmas. Her mother took one look at the daughter she had given up for dead and promptly fainted. Marketa found out that her father had been in a concentration camp, where he had suffered terribly. Now he was shipping coal and her mother was working in a printing factory. Her parents agreed to hitchhike back to Paris with Marketa.

In France Marta awaited them, and the reduced Naičova family was reunited.

Before Marketa's hurried trip to Czechoslovakia, she had met Lt. Col. George Kimbrell. They fell in love, and in 1949 George and Marketa were married (Marta ultimately married his best friend). Shortly after, Kimbrell was ordered to return to America, and in 1950 the couple settled in Los Angeles, California.

Within four years Marketa had three infant sons, her husband was sent to Korea, returned safely, and was killed in an automobile accident. Her parents came from France to help take care of the children, and Marketa resumed her acting career to support the family. She was twenty-six.

Work was plentiful on television and there were many parts for an attractive, talented young woman with an interesting accent. People began to pay attention to her talent when she starred as an important witness in a ninety-minute show called "Judgment at Nuremberg" depicting the much publicized war criminal trials. The director, George Roy Hill, wrote her a letter telling her, "I think you are one of the most remarkably talented actresses I have ever come across in this medium. I also think you have a great future. . . ." Film director Stanley Kramer sent her a note telling her that her performance was wonderful.

She was acclaimed for her starring role in a theater production of *Saint Joan*, in which she toured the country. This tour took her to New York, where she did more television and appeared in some Broadway productions including one called *The Wall*, which depicted the struggle of the Jews in the Polish ghetto during World War II. She had left her boys, who were then nine, eleven, and twelve, with her parents. The grandparents spoke no English and the boys spoke no Czech. "It was disastrous," recalls Marketa. "I never left them again."

Deciding that her career would flourish best in New York, she bought a large house on Long Island with the insurance money she had received from her husband's death. In 1961 she brought her family to their new home.

In 1962 Marketa joined the Living Theater, which was run by political activists Julian Beck and Judith Malina. With them she participated in nonviolent street demonstrations and hunger strikes protesting nuclear arms, our Cuban policy, and in 1964, against the war in Vietnam. A couple of times she was arrested. Because of her activities, and partly, she thinks, because of her friendships with people who were blacklisted during the McCarthy period, she began to feel a subtle blacklist of herself as a television actress and some not-so-subtle attacks in the theater.

However, one director didn't join in the blacklist. Sidney Lumet cast her in the movie *The Pawnbroker,* where she gave a poignant portrayal of Rod Steiger's German Jewish mistress.

In 1967 she joined the Lincoln Center repertory company. Her antiwar sentiments made her a target of harassment by stagehands. Peace signs, which she put up in her dressing room, were torn down. She was even threatened physically.

By then, she says, she was not only sick of the attacks, she was fed up with the caliber of the work. Gathering a handful of actors together, she formed her own company. Her first production, in a tiny East Village theater, was a program of poems by the Spanish writer Garcia Lorca expressing views of New York City. Many of her actors were very young or very old nonprofessionals, yet the production was moving and effective and earned some praising reviews.

But Marketa was not looking for big-time acceptance. "I had this thing in me about going to poor people. I had a need to reach the people nobody touched." With some money from the New York Council on the Arts, the company took a show through the New York ghettos. "I had never seen poverty up close before," Marketa confides. "I had seen people made poor by war, but this was inherited poverty. Once in the ghetto, I was forcibly reminded who society's victims are. I was immediately drawn to working with them."

The play Marketa chose to produce was Bertolt Brecht's *Exception and the Rule.* In it a coolie and his master, the merchant, are lost in the desert. The merchant has abused the coolie, whipping him and forcing him to carry their belongings. Now lost and without water, the merchant begins to imagine that the coolie will kill him. When the coolie weakly extends to the parched merchant a flask of water that he has kept concealed, the merchant, thinking he is being attacked, shoots the coolie and kills him. In the final trial scene, the coolie's family asks for justice. The merchant is found not guilty. The reason given is that in their society, where the poor are oppressed, the rule would be that the coolie would kill the merchant. Therefore, the merchant was following the rule and shooting in self-defense. It was not his fault that this time was the exception.

By 1970 the company had received $21,000 in combined grants from the Rockefeller brothers, the New York Council on the Arts, and the New York Foundation to tour the country. They were able to find a large, deserted building in Coney Island in which to rehearse. After considerable effort to make the barren warehouse-type room habitable, the actors began to look for a play. *The Bremen Town Musicians,* by the brothers Grimm, became the basis of their production.

In this play, an old donkey who can no longer haul sacks to the mill is thrown out by his master. He decides to go to Bremen Town and earn his living as a street musician. Along the way he meets a dog, a cat, and a rooster. All have been rejected by their masters. They decide to join the donkey.

They go through a dark forest. The rooster, from a perch in a tree, sees a light, and the animals go off to find its source. They come to a robber's den. Through the window they see the robbers eating a large meal. The animals pile on top of each other and begin to sing for their supper. Then they fall through the window. The robbers are so terrified by the awful noise and this seemingly tall monster that they flee into the woods. The animals enjoy some of the food and go to sleep.

Meanwhile, one of the robbers goes back to see what frightened them. It is dark when he enters the house. Thinking the cat's eyes are glowing coals, he starts to strike a match on them. The cat scratches him. The man runs to the door, where the dog bites him, and into the yard, where the donkey kicks him. During all this the rooster is crowing loudly.

The robber stumbles back to his friends to tell them that the house is full of demons, and the robbers decide never to go back. The animals stay and live happily ever after.

The actors began their work by each of them trying to play the various animals. This is what they ended up with: The donkey, a black worker from the south, is thrown out by the master. He heads for New York City, where he figures he'll have to go on welfare. As he travels, he sings a song that he learned from the sharecroppers. A Puerto Rican dog, an Appalachian cat, and an Indian rooster join him. They all decide to go to New York and try to cut a record.

The robber's den is called Washington Inc., and the feast the robbers are having is a fund-raising banquet. The play's ending has the animals sharing their bounty with all the other hungry creatures.

Wherever the company went that first year, the people responded enthusiastically. They begged Marketa and her actors to come back to them, and Marketa promised she would. It's a commitment she doesn't take lightly.

For the company, it was not only a theatrical and ideological experience, it was a fantastic chance to touch many facets of American life.

At the Navajo reservation in Chinle, Arizona, the actors performed to an almost nonexistent audience. The next day people came up to them and told them how much they loved the play. The mystery was, How did the Navajos see the show and how many actually did? They never found out.

In Detroit the company set up their equipment on the lawn of a housing project. There were a few old black people sitting apathetically on the lawn, not to watch the show but as an evening custom. When the performers started their tape recorder with Robert Johnson of the Delta Blues Singers doing "You Better Come in My Kitchen, There's Gonna Be Rainin' Outdoors," the old people became animated. One very old woman suddenly jumped up and started dancing. "Hot dog!" she cried. The actors immediately went forward and helped the old people move their chairs closer to the stage. They had an audience.

At the Cheyenne reservation in Lame Deer, Montana, the troupe was advised that there was growing hostility in the tribe between full-breeds and half-breeds with especial dislike for blacks. This worried the actors, because in their production a black actor was playing the Indian. They performed with misgivings and at the end were surprised and thrilled by the roar of approval that went through the audience.

Hearing of a massive strike being organized in Salinas, California, by the United Farm Workers, the company decided to stop there and perhaps perform afterwards. Thousands of Mexican American men and women attended the evening meeting, which lasted four hours. The actors were enormously moved by the strength and unity of the people and began to feel that their play would be extraneous after such an historic event. Marketa explained (with one of the Spanish members translating) that since it was late and the workers had to get up early to picket, they would postpone their performance to another time. But the people shouted, *"Ahora! Ahora!* Now! Now!" and of course, the company performed.

There was a performance for the coal miners in West Virginia, where after the show the miners and actors gathered together and the miners talked of the outrages and humiliations that they were forced to endure. They only hoped that the actors would take their story to the outside world, where, as Marketa commented dryly, "Surely there will be justice."

The 1971 tour was even more successful. They had a year's experience behind them and a new play, *The Mother*, which was extremely well received (it was written by Marketa after having read Maxim Gorky's novel *The Mother* and Bertold Brecht's play, which was adapted from the novel). Marketa composed much of her own dialogue. She also used dialogue from George Jackson's book *Soledad Brother*. It was the first year that Marketa participated as an actress as well as a director. In 1971 the company also began doing performances in prisons. The warden at Sing Sing wrote Marketa ". . . *The Mother* was a very poignant and pertinent performance to which all the men were able to relate. . . ." From the warden of the North Carolina Prison she received the following: ". . .Your production of *The Mother* was a moving, inspiring experience for all the men who live here. . . ."

It's a spring day. Marketa, in her usual pants and work shirt, sits in the pleasant living room of her large Tudor house. Outside, the lawn is neatly cut, and the rhododendron bushes are in full bloom. Several cats can be seen sunning themselves in the driveway and on the porch steps and railing. Inside the house dogs roam from room to room, crowding around a visitor, looking for affection. (Marketa still cares for homeless, sick animals, as in her childhood, and her home generally has ten to twenty dogs, cats, rabbits, and other animals in residence.)

The furnishings in the house are of no particular style or period. The furniture seems to have been chosen for comfort rather than fashion. The living room boasts many books and a large grand piano, which Andy, the youngest son, who wants to be a concert pianist, uses for practicing.

Marketa's father died a few years ago. Her mother, a diminutive woman with a limited English vocabulary, still lives with her and today is bustling about the house.

Andy, in his early twenties, and Mark, two years older, are going out to play tennis. They are tall, handsome men who are close with their mother and share her political views.

Marketa is getting ready for another summer tour. In talking about her goals, it is difficult for her to say what she feels she can accomplish. With no illusions that she can change society, she does feel, nevertheless, that the communication between different parts of society is important.

"I guess my ultimate goal is to create such a theater in style and meaning and communication that it is loved and accepted by the people I care about. I want a real theater. Perhaps my group will be one small step toward creating a national theater in this country. I have two needs: to reach the people and to express myself theatrically. I'm always looking for new forms. Now I'm working with masks. I have an idea of having a character use a mask part of the time and when he takes it off it's like a closeup in a film.

"It's important to me that our theater never be second rate. I don't want the poor to think we come to them because we're not wanted elsewhere.

"I know I'm not doing enough work, but I'm still held back by habit and routine. My home, my garden, my family, my animals all make demands on me. Then, as an actress there's a conflict. It's sometimes gloriously exciting to walk into a commercial play with no responsibility, just to perform.

"There is so much I want to accomplish and I'm always afraid I won't continue to have the strength. Every time we enter a migrant camp or an Indian reservation, it's a challenge. Will we succeed in communicating? I worry about bringing a radical play to a reactionary world. I worry about taking out the company alone. I quake before each prison workshop, wondering if I'll be able to hold their attention, to make it worthwhile for them. I have to be careful with the inmates' feelings. They so easily consider themselves inadequate. One of my favorite men gave me a play he had written and asked me what I thought of it. I gave him the mildest criticism, but he couldn't even take that. He was very upset and hasn't returned to the workshop. It's a real loss.

"I guess my need to try in some small way to help the helpless, to cry out against injustice, can be explained by an incident from my childhood. One day from the window of my home in Prague, I saw a long line of Jews being marched off to a concentration camp. I started to scream. My mother, terrified that the Nazis would hear me, rushed over and hit me so hard that I passed out. I think what my mother stopped in me then is coming out now. I only know theater, so I'll cry out through my plays. There's a lot of pain in that childhood memory. Unless I participate now, unlike what I did then, I keep repeating that part of history. I can't live with it twice."

Eleanor Holmes Norton

In April 1970 an attractive thirty-two-year-old lawyer named Eleanor Holmes Norton became the commissioner of human rights for New York City. She was the first black woman to be chosen to head the city's most powerful anti-discrimination agency.

The appointment didn't come as a surprise to anyone who had been following the swiftly moving career of the brilliant young attorney. For the past five years, as a lawyer for the American Civil Liberties Union (ACLU), she had distinguished herself by successfully defending the right to free speech for such diversified personalities as black Georgia state congressman Julian Bond and segregationist George Wallace.

She had become famous for her absolute reverence for the first amendment of the Constitution which guarantees free, peaceful expression for all Americans. She was available to defend anyone, regardless of their views, if their civil rights were threatened.

Ms. Norton was born Eleanor Holmes on June 13, 1937, in Washington, D.C. Her father was a Washington bureaucrat and her mother was a teacher. She was the oldest of three girls. "We were a close family and an egalitarian family," she says in the well-modulated voice that occasionally takes on a Southern inflection. "My father always

wanted a boy but never seemed fazed that he had all girls. He was terribly proud of us and just assumed that girls could do whatever boys did. My mother and grandmother felt the same way, and my sisters and I had a sense that a little girl can grow up to be somebody."

Young Eleanor developed strong feelings against injustice and oppression. The subject of segregation was constantly discussed in her family. She went to segregated schools (she graduated in 1955, and the schools in Washington were de-segregated in 1954), and she became aware that about the only facilities blacks could share with whites in the country's capital were seats on the city busses. "If you were black," recalls Ms. Norton, "you could have a charge account at a department store, but you couldn't use the toilet."

Despite the constant public humiliations, the black middle-class families in Washington protected their children against feelings of inferiority. "Our parents always let us know," she remembers, "that the kind of white people who would have segregation were ignorant, perverse people whom none of us would wish to be like. We were made to feel that we were the superior ones."

As a small girl Eleanor cherished the notion of becoming a missionary in Africa. "Then I grew up," she says smiling, "and in the sixth grade I wanted to be a teacher like all the nice little colored girls wanted to be." In high school she found she had a flair for writing and decided her future was in journalism. She changed her mind again in her first year at Antioch College. Science was the new interest, and she seriously considered a career in medicine. By the end of her second year she realized that her intense interest in social justice made law the most logical career for herself.

Eleanor attended Yale Law School, where she received her degree in law as well as a master's degree in American studies. In 1964 she went from Yale to Philadelphia to clerk for a federal judge for one year. "A clerkship," she explains, "is like graduate training."

It was during her clerking period that she met her future husband, Edward Norton, who was in the navy and stationed in Philadelphia.

Edward was attracted to the young lawyer precisely because she was self-sufficient and ambitious. "He liked the fact that I was a highly educated woman," she recalls. "Nobody would have married me who didn't want a woman with a career. By the time my husband met me, a career was totally built into my being. I would never have attracted a man who wanted a wife to stay home."

The couple was married in Eleanor's grandfather's backyard on October 9, 1965, four months after they had met.

The Nortons came to New York where Edward enrolled in Columbia Law School and Eleanor got a job with the American Civil Liberties Union.

"I was basically a first amendment expert," she recalls. "It was the time of the Vietnam war, it was the time of the civil rights movement, it was a time when people were trying to establish their right to protest at all. I represented criminals and protesters and civil rights activists."

It was during her five years with ACLU that Eleanor demonstrated the strength of her belief in the first amendment. When the National States Rights Party (NSRP), an unabashedly white supremicist party, held a rally in Princess Anne, Maryland, in August 1966, caustic language was used by the speakers in describing black people. Despite the fact that there was no violence at the rally, an injunction was issued against the party barring it from holding a rally in the county again for ten days. Although disagreeing with everything the NSRP stood for, the ACLU felt the injunction against them was unconstitutional. Eleanor argued the case and won.

When a member of the NSRP came up afterward to tell

Eleanor what an excellent job she had done and that she had shown a lot of guts in taking the case, Eleanor quickly explained that guts had nothing to do with it. "I told him," she recalls, "that it was simply my organization's commitment to the first amendment. He just smiled. I still don't know if he realized what I was saying."

In 1968, when New York's mayor, John V. Lindsay, tried to prevent segregationist George Wallace from speaking in Shea Stadium, Eleanor again successfully took up the cudgels for free speech. "The point is," she says, "if people like George Wallace are denied free expression, then the same thing can happen to black people. Black people understand this. No black person ever said to me, 'Sister how come you're representing George Wallace?' They knew how come."

There were cases closer to the young lawyer's heart. One such case involved the black Georgia state congressman Julian Bond.

In 1965 Bond was elected to the Georgia legislature. In 1966 a move began on the part of some members of the House to bar him from his elected seat because of his outspoken criticism of the Vietnam war and the military draft.

When the Georgia House of Representatives voted 184 to 12 to deny Julian Bond his seat, the ACLU came in and asked the United States Supreme Court to overrule the House vote. The Supreme Court unanimously ruled that Julian Bond's constitutional rights were violated when the House refused to seat him. It was another victory for the first amendment.

Ms. Norton makes it clear that she did not go to court on this particular case. She was simply one of a team of lawyers who drew up the brief.

Eleanor had no idea that she was being considered for the job of commissioner of human rights during the year of

1969. "I hadn't been involved in the Lindsay administration in any way," she explains. "In fact, on the George Wallace issue, I had opposed the mayor. Then one day a woman in the city government called me up and said she was going to propose my name for commissioner. I laughed at her. I had never thought of myself as a person on the inside of government. Then I began to hear from more and more people that I was being considered for the job. Finally, I began to hear it from important people in the administration."

When she was offered the job, Eleanor was hesitant about taking it. She wondered if there might be some basic compromise involved in working on the inside of government. All her training had been geared toward working for the people, not for the bureaucracy. Since the Human Rights Commission was established to represent complainants—to provide lawyers for them and then to process the complaints—she decided there was no compromise.

She had also had an opportunity to see the effectiveness of the commission in action. A year before, she and her husband, while apartment-hunting, saw an ad in the paper for a rent-controlled apartment that sounded perfect for their needs. They called the landlord, who asked them about themselves. "We told him we were both lawyers and that we had no children," recalls Ms. Norton. "The man was delighted and told us to come down immediately and leave a deposit and that the apartment could be ours. We did, and a few hours later the landlord called and told us someone else had gotten the apartment. Obviously he didn't want black tenants, even if they were lawyers. My husband said to him, 'The next time you hear from us will be through the Human Rights Commission.' Then we went down and filed a complaint. The landlord didn't want to have trouble with the commission, and we got the apartment."

In April 1970, Eleanor Holmes Norton became the

highest ranking black woman in the Lindsay administration. Her job, she told an interviewer from the *New York Times*, was to make sure "that no man is judged by the irrational criteria of race, religion, or national origin." She then added, "And I assure you I use the word *man* in the generic sense, for I mean to do all I can to see that the principle of nondiscrimination becomes a reality for women as well."

As commissioner, Eleanor's life became an active one. Her daughter, Katherine, was born on July 9, 1970, and after four weeks at home Eleanor was back at work. Each morning before going to her office, the new mother would take her baby up to Harlem to her mother-in-law's house, and each night she would pick her up before going home. Her days were filled with phone calls, hearings, speeches, and administrative duties. Instead of being periods of relaxation, lunch hours were often times to make speeches, and it was a rare day that she didn't stay in the office at least an hour after her secretary had gone home.

True to her word, the new commissioner was busy rooting out every possible form of discrimination. She chaired hearings on job discrimination against returning Vietnam veterans, ex-offenders, and people over forty. Her commission called on the carpet large corporations that had discriminatory hiring practices against women and minorities. Ms. Norton observed, "Most people think civil rights today is about 'whether or not I'm turning down somebody at the door because he is black or female.' It doesn't happen that way anymore. It is more subtle. It happens when women are asked at a job interview, 'Do you intend to get pregnant within the next two years?' And it happens to women much more than it happens to blacks, because blacks have spent 300 years trying to educate the country about how perverse it all is."

Commissioner Norton also had hearings on school hiring practices in New York City. "It was incredible to me," she says, "that New York was the only school system in the United States that managed not to employ blacks. Teaching is the one profession for which blacks have historically been prepared." As a result of the hearings, more black teachers were hired in the New York schools.

When Commissioner Norton conducted a census of city government, she generated some consternation among the employees. Civil service and Jewish groups were distrustful because they thought the census would result in their being weeded out of their government jobs. "I made it clear," explains Eleanor Norton, "that the only way to find out if there is discrimination in government is to find out if there are any blacks, Puerto Ricans, or women employed. The census was simply to find the facts, not to deprive people of employment. I also let them know that our census had good civil liberties protection. I'm happy to say that when the census was published, there was no controversy.

On March 17, 1972, a second child, John Holmes Norton, was born. Again Eleanor took off four weeks, and when she went back to work she was leaving both children, daily, with her mother-in-law. However, by then the Nortons had purchased a large town house in Harlem, so transporting the children became simpler. A year later, she and her husband employed someone to take care of the children five days a week at home.

Eleanor Norton was once asked by a journalist if she ever felt cheated of spending time with her children. "I sure never felt cheated of spending time with John," she answered laughing. "He didn't sleep straight through the night for six months, and I always got up with him when he would wake up at 3:00 or 4:00 A.M. He and I had plenty of time together." She went on to say that she always makes sure that she allots time after work for her children. "I set aside two hours each night just to be with the kids," she said. "If I have work from the office to do, I don't start it until after the kids are in bed. I generally work until midnight, and I get up at 7:30."

The Nortons have always tried to maintain an equal partnership in terms of work and the children. Sometimes, however, traditional ways of doing things take over. For example, in 1973 Commissioner Norton was conducting two days of hearings on housing in New York City. The first day was off to a good start with Mayor Lindsay seated next to the commissioner. Flash bulbs popped, radio stations were broadcasting the hearings, and reporters from the major newspapers were present.

After making an opening speech, the mayor left, and Commissioner Norton proceeded with the hearings, calling on witnesses and questioning them at length. At one point in the day a gentleman came in and whispered in her ear. She immediately got up from her chair and said to the assemblage, "Please excuse me. I've just received a call that my son is sick. I must go to the phone." She turned the chair over to someone else and left. Twenty minutes later she was back and told the people at the hearing that her son was fine and she was sorry for the delay.

Later, in recounting the incident, Ms. Norton said, "On the phone, I asked the sitter, 'Why on earth didn't you call Edward?' [Edward was and still is general counsel for the New York Housing Authority.] Do you know, it never entered her mind. She was conditioned to call the mother. It didn't occur to her to call the person who might be less busy at the moment."

Toward the end of 1973, as John Lindsay's term of office was coming to an end, Commissioner Eleanor Holmes Norton, though uncertain whether she would be asked to stay on in the next administration, was still working toward ending discrimination in New York. Her aim was an integrated New York City. She had gotten out of the legislature a tough antiblockbusting law. This meant that she was in a position to go after real estate people who came into neighborhoods where blacks were moving in and panicked the white people into selling and running to the suburbs. "People run from neighborhoods because they have no idea what black people are like," says Commissioner Norton. "They think black people live in Harlem and are on welfare and, 'Lord, some of them are going to move next to me, so I'm going to move to the suburbs.' The point is," she continues, her eyes flashing, "the black who moves next door to you is most likely to be a policeman whose wife is a nurse, and together they make $25,000. It's a great financial sacrifice for them to move out of the ghetto and they're going to work hard to keep the new neighborhood from becoming another ghetto."

Ms. Norton believes equally as strongly in improving the ghettos. In 1971 the Nortons found a beautiful house in Harlem. Edward Norton, who was born in the black ghetto, was wary about returning to it, but since the house was everything they could want in a home, he agreed to make the move.

"As it turns out," says Eleanor Norton, "we live on a nice block. I hadn't planted a flower in my whole life, but come spring, I had my petunias out." She laughs warmly. "Now why did I have my petunias out? Because the lady next door had her petunias out. That's the way it happens on a block. I take care of my grass and care about my block because everyone else does."

Along with her work as commissioner of human rights, Eleanor Norton had been continually active in the women's movement, so it was only natural that when the National Black Feminist Organization came into being in August 1973, she was named as one of its founders. In October of that year she gave a speech to the Publicity Club of New York and talked about why black women needed their own organization. She explained that black women have different problems from their white sisters. "Blacks must re-make the family situation," she said. "We need a strong family unit as it was before slavery." She also expressed the fear that blacks will ape the traditional white family situation where men are the financial heads of the family and stated that the problem hinges on the black woman finding herself outside the home. At the end of her speech, she said eloquently, "No one writes about black women—what's in their heads, what's in their hearts."

In February 1974 the new mayor of New York City, Abraham Beame, announced that Eleanor Holmes Norton would continue as commissioner of human rights.

Eleanor Holmes Norton sits behind her large, modern, glass-topped desk in her airy office. There are handsome contemporary paintings on the white walls, and the tables and the desk are adorned with vases of dried flowers and pictures of her husband and two children. There is also a picture of the commissioner and Coretta King. On a cabinet behind the desk is a stunning piece of sculpture of a black woman holding a baby.

Whenever Eleanor Holmes Norton talks about her work and her ideals, she inevitably returns to the subject of the first amendment. It is then that she becomes most passionate.

"When Martin Luther King broke open the civil rights question in relation to masses of people in the late fifties," she begins, "it was because he could say what he wished to say. In going to jail, he had access to a legal system of which some fairness could ultimately be wrenched—although in his case, not until the Supreme Court became involved. It is precisely when the first amendment has not operated that blacks have been most oppressed and suppressed. For example, in the twenties, when so many blacks were lynched and you couldn't talk to a white women in a certain way.

Then the first amendment was not operative. The ordinary amenities of social expression brought terror to the hearts of blacks. Then in the sixties, blacks went from feeling totally inferior to a feeling of being full and whole and beautiful people. That was because of free expression. Wow!" The commissioner's dark eyes glow with excitement. "When you think about free expression, you think about the Watergate hearings. That's all about free expression.

"You have to have contempt for the minds of men if you think you can't ultimately get at the truth by hearing opposing sides. Some people think free expression leads to violence. There *are* some occasions when some speaker works people up, but that's very rare. Speech isn't what leads to violence. Free speech can avoid violence. If civil rights hadn't come by free expression, it would probably have come by revolution.

"I'm in love with the first amendment because I think it's such a beautiful, flowing mechanism. Most of my studying was in history, and I've studied with some great people. All are impressed with the importance of the first amendment in promoting almost every social change, at least in the twentieth century. There's the labor movement, the women's movement, and the civil rights movement—all these began with protest. When you think about it, you just have to cherish the first amendment."

Eleanor Norton goes on to talk about the difficulties of working and raising a family. "I was lucky," she says. "First of all, my mother-in-law is marvelous. She gave my children all the love and affection I could have wished for them. Secondly, because of my job, I have a city car at my disposal, so I don't have to take my children back and forth by public transportation. For most women, it's much harder. My whole position on working women is that women ought to have choices. The choices are not always available to women today. Without day care centers, without equal employment opportunities, the right to work is more mythical than real."

Eleanor Holmes Norton is happy about continuing her job under the new administration, but it's clear that she will never compromise her ideals. "If the government is pushing for new frontiers and for civil rights and problems of the city," she says, "then government is the place for me to be. If it is not," she concludes with finality, "then it is not the place for me."

Eve Queler

On a December evening in 1973, a standing-room-only crowd at New York's Carnegie Hall waited expectantly for the opening bars of a concert version of Georges Bizet's seldom performed opera *The Pearl Fishers*. The importance of the evening was marked by some of the illustrious people in the audience—Grace Bumbry of Metropolitan Opera fame, and Julius Rudel, conductor of the New York City Opera.

At 8:00 P.M. the singers filed onstage. Metropolitan Opera tenor Nicolai Gedda received a fantastic ovation. And then, the person responsible for the whole event, conductor Eve Queler, founder and music director of the Opera Orchestra of New York, made an entrance to even louder applause.

For those who envision conductors as men in white tie and tails, Eve's appearance is something of a shock. She is a slim, five-foot four-inch young woman with long, jet black hair and a sweet, small-featured face. For the *Pearl Fishers* performance she was dressed in a cherry red, floor-length gown that complemented her hair and the fairness of her skin.

When the applause had subsided, Eve picked up the baton, and if there had been any doubts that this woman could manage a large orchestra, they were soon dispelled.

She displayed a strength and assurance that the orchestra and singers easily responded to. The evening was a smashing success, and when the last haunting note of this beautiful opera had died away, there were bravos and a stamping of feet.

The next day the *New York Times* music critic, Harold Schonberg, after complimenting Eve on the handling of the music, wrote, "In short, she is a fine conductor, which will come as no surprise to those who have been following her work in the last few years."

When she was asked if she was pleased by Schonberg's praise, Eve answered, "I never read reviews." The truth is she was too busy. She was already at work studying the score of Bellini's *I Puritani*, which she would conduct, in concert, for her London debut in February 1974. Then back to Philadelphia to conduct Berlioz's *Damnation of Faust* on February 19. From there she would return to New York to prepare for her second Carnegie Hall concert of the season on March 6.

Hardly a newcomer to the world of music, Eve, whose maiden name is Eve Rabin, began taking piano lessons during the 1940s when she was only five years old.

The Rabins were lower middle-class hard-working New Yorkers with very little money, but they recognized a talent in their youngest daughter and were able to secure a piano scholarship for her that lasted until she was twelve years old.

Once Eve started her lessons, music became her whole life. Every day after school she practiced the piano before she did anything else. Much of her childhood was spent giving concerts and entering piano contests. She had a dedication, and it set her apart from her friends. "And yet," she says, "my friends accepted this obsession I had. They never made me feel particularly different from them. I guess I managed to have a good time, too."

If Eve did find times to have fun, they must have come at odd moments, for her recollections are primarily of work. Her father had a small factory where he cut and packaged French imported cheese. As soon as she was old enough, Eve was spending her Saturdays working in the factory to earn a little money. Later she graduated to baby-sitting jobs and playing the piano in a ballet studio and in Sunday school.

Eve recalls, "There was no notion in our house that girls grow up and have careers. The reason both my sister and I have careers [Eve's sister is a school principal] is very simple. First of all, there was very little excitement in our home, so my sister and I were eager to get out and do other things. Secondly, there wasn't any money. Both of us were motivated at a very early age to look after our own needs. For example, I never had any clothes, except for the ones my sister was finished with. When my scholarship was over and piano lessons had to be paid for, I was responsible for them. When it was time to wear braces on my teeth, I took care of the orthodontist bills. By the time I was sixteen, I was completely on my own financially."

The orthodontist bills were more of a financial burden than she had anticipated. "When I needed braces," remembers Eve, "I didn't ask my father. I simply went to the dentist and said, 'What do you think of these teeth?' He said I needed braces and sent me to an orthodontist. Everything was settled, except what I could pay. At that point I brought in my mother and the orthodontist asked her what we could afford to pay per month. My mother, being naive, told him an amount that was exactly what I made every month." Eve laughs at the memory. "In her innocence she strapped me into giving up all my earnings."

When she graduated from high school, Eve decided to take a year off before going on to college. She was eager to practice the piano seven hours a day instead of wedging it in between homework and part-time jobs. She was sure she would be a concert pianist and wanted the time to direct all her energies toward that goal.

It was a good year, and when it was over Eve was back in school—two schools, in fact. She enrolled in both the City College of New York and Mannes Music School. Saturdays she worked at a lingerie store. She says she must have been practicing a great deal during that period, because she recalls giving a concert.

It was at C.C.N.Y. that Eve met her future husband, Stanley Queler. "I met him practically the minute I walked in the door," she says. "He was a senior and I was a freshman."

Stanley didn't have much money either, but he did manage to buy his lunch at school. Not Eve. Every day she brought her lunch in a brown paper bag. "I always ate the same thing," she says smiling. "Sandwiches made with Gruyère cheese from my father's factory. Stanley laughed at my lunches, but he grew to adore Gruyère cheese sandwiches."

In those days at C.C.N.Y. most of the students came from poor families. It was a free city college with high scholastic requirements, and all the students had to work as Eve did. "In fact," she remembers, "I was one of the luckier ones. A lot of my friends had to contribute money to the home. I was able to keep what I made."

When Eve went into her second year at C.C.N.Y., Stanley left for law school. Soon after, Eve decided that attending two schools was more than she could manage. She quit C.C.N.Y. and finished all her courses at Mannes. She continued to practice and to work at odd jobs such as playing the organ in churches and temples.

In the middle of Stanley's second year of law school, he and Eve decided to get married.

"I said to myself," remembers Eve, 'You're making the

biggest mistake, because you'll never practice.' All I thought about was that I would have to keep on working and that Stanley was in law school and that neither of us had any money. I was sure I would have to give up my career because I wouldn't be able to practice."

As it turned out, she *was* able to practice, and she did continue doing odd jobs. They couldn't afford piano lessons for her, but at that point she didn't mind. "I had been taking lessons since I was five," she says, "and it was time to stop and think about what I was doing and what I was playing."

Actually, she was beginning to give up the idea of becoming a concert pianist and was developing an interest in accompanying singers. "It had nothing to do with being married," she emphasizes. "It had more to do with the fact that I was really not temperamentally suited to solo work. I didn't have the kind of nerves needed to be a soloist. Every time I gave a concert I had a lot of nightmares before it. I dreamed that I was going to trip and die and everything. And quite honestly, I was not that good a pianist. I just wouldn't have made it."

Her decision to accompany came from her growing love for *lieder* (German songs) and opera. She began getting jobs accompanying singers, including a fairly important position accompanying a leading baritone, Martial Singher.

In 1957 the Quelers' first child, Andrew, was born. Six months later Eve was hired as a rehearsal accompanist and coach for the New York City Opera. It was her big opportunity.

By that time Stanley was practicing law but was still earning very little money. Eve's salary was so low that everything she made paid for a housekeeper to take care of Andy while she was at work. At night she walked the floor with her infant, who was going through a painful teething bout.

"It was a terrible time," recalls Eve. "I was working seven days and seven nights a week. I didn't have any time to sleep or practice the things I needed to learn for the job. I didn't know very many operas, and I still wasn't that good at sight-reading music. As a soloist you can prepare yourself, but as an accompanist you have to do a lot of sight-reading, and there are no second chances. It was hard times," she adds grimly. "If you can't sleep, you can't do your work. That season there were thirteen operas, and I only knew *Traviata.*"

In 1958, at the end of her first season with the City Opera, Eve was not asked to come back for the following year. She was told that her sight-reading wasn't good enough and that they needed someone with more experience. She was absolutely crushed. "I felt like I had my big chance and lost it," she says. "It was terribly painful."

Despite the miserable sense of failure, she determined that she would practice until she learned all the scores and was an excellent sight-reader. "Then," she told herself, "they'll ask me back." And they did—but not for seven years.

In the meantime she was busy growing and learning. She accompanied and coached at the Metropolitan Opera Studio and the Metropolitan National Company and even started an opera workshop. In 1960 she took time out to have another baby—a daughter, Elizabeth.

In 1965, as she had predicted, City Opera asked Eve to come back again as coach and accompanist. She accepted. But by then she had started toying with the idea of becoming a conductor and had gone back to Mannes to study the technique with two excellent teachers. She was moving into this new phase very slowly.

"It was hard to make a decision to become a conductor," recalls Eve. "Women weren't doing conducting in those days; and besides, I didn't know what kind of ability I had.

I felt I really had to evaluate my potentials. After all, I wasn't a kid anymore. I was a married woman, I had two children and a lot of responsibilities. I thought I could do it. I knew I had a good ear and many other attributes that should make a conductor, but I wasn't sure."

One means of testing her conducting ability was through the Opera Orchestra of New York, which Eve founded in 1967. Her initial intention in starting the orchestra was to provide a place for student instrumentalists to learn the operatic repertory. There were numerous conservatories where musicians could learn symphonic works but few institutions for studying opera.

At first the orchestra only rehearsed. Then, wanting an audience, Eve conducted the musicians in a concert version of an opera in a junior high school auditorium. She used singers who were young and talented but still unacclaimed. As the orchestra continued to perform, it moved to more and more prestigious halls, and in 1972 it made its debut at Carnegie Hall, where it has been performing ever since.

Through the years the composition of the orchestra has changed, as has the stature of the singers. The student musicians have been replaced by highly professional instrumentalists, and the leading singers, instead of being young people on the way up, are Metropolitan Opera stars.

There have been times when the use of stars proved to be a mixed blessing. When Eve made her Carnegie Hall debut with the opera *William Tell* by Rossini, her tenor was Metropolitan Opera star Nicolai Gedda. He is a beloved singer and a good portion of the audience had come expressly to hear him sing an enormously difficult role. A day and a half before the night of performance, Gedda became ill, and it was clear he would not be well enough to sing. Undaunted, Eve recruited two other tenors to replace the star (the role was too difficult for one man to learn on such short notice). One would sing the first half of the opera and the other, the second half. She worked with both men, coaching them throughout the day until performance time. Then she had the thankless task of going out and explaining to her expectant audience that the singer they had come to hear would not perform that evening. There was tremendous disappointment, but the audience stayed to cheer a highly successful evening. Eve's conducting was described by one critic as "inspired."

There have been other crises that Eve has taken in stride. She is not only the conductor of the orchestra but is also the concerned mother to her musicians and singers. When her tenor had a cold before one performance, Eve rushed him off to the doctor to ensure that he would be able to go on. Another time, the baritone, who was flying from Italy to work with her, had his plane flight delayed and came a day late for rehearsal. Unflustered, Eve canceled a fitting for the gown she was to wear for the performance to work with the baritone. "I'll wear one of my old dresses," she said philosophically. "People will have to put up with seeing me in a gown I've worn before. The music is more important than clothes."

Although she still continues to do opera in concert form, Eve has changed in her choice of material to be presented. Originally she performed the standard scores that everyone knew and loved. Now that she is more secure, she feels freer to choose obscure operas that are rarely done.

Eve remembers that even though she was constantly working with the Opera Orchestra of New York, she didn't list herself as a conductor on her résumé until the fall of 1970, when she had her first post as an associate conductor at Fort Wayne, Indiana.

In many ways Eve came into her own during the year at Fort Wayne. Not only was she the associate conductor of the Fort Wayne, Indiana, Philharmonic, but she was able to originate a children's participation series in which she explained the construction of a piece of music to her audience. It turned out to be a huge success with adults as well as children.

"When you understand how a piece is built," Eve told a reporter, "music is fascinating as well as enjoyable. I find that appreciation goes up in proportion to the audience's understanding." Then she added, "This understanding needn't be technical. I gave explanations at nearly every concert and never once used a technical term."

She was also eager to show her audiences that a conductor does more than beat time. "The role of the conductor," she explained, "is to balance the orchestra—to interpret the music and coordinate the musicians so that they complement one another within the boundaries of the score."

Eve's move to Indiana had a profound effect on the Quelers' home life. Stanley and the two children stayed in New York during that year while Eve had an apartment in Fort Wayne. If she had a week off, she would come to New York, and her family would come to Indiana during school and summer vacations.

"And it worked," Eve says. "It worked because the family decided it must work. Stanley understood that I had to do this in order to establish myself as a conductor. It gave him a chance to know the children, and although I had a housekeeper, he had to do a great deal. He had to run the house, he had to make lunches for the kids each morning. He and the children became very close. I think it was good for all of us. For the first time in my life I had an apartment of my own and a chance to be alone." She smiles at the memory. "I liked it."

At the end of the season in 1971, Eve decided that to stay on in Indiana would mean moving her whole family there, and she realized that she didn't want to make her home in Fort Wayne. Besides, she had assignments to guest conduct the French National Radio Orchestra in Paris, the Boston Philharmonic, and a Mozart Festival at Philharmonic Hall in New York. It was time to put *conductor* on her résumé.

Eve has come a long way from the pianist who panicked before every concert. As a conductor, nervousness is forgotten in her concern for the orchestra and the singers. During rehearsals she is totally without temperament and will patiently go over and over a section of music until she is satisfied that it is as good as it can be. If a singer needs extra coaching, she is available to help him or her at any odd hour.

When Eve picks up the baton to conduct, she commands a great deal of respect and admiration. Her conducting is simple and strong and she avoids the dramatic gyrations that some of her male colleagues use. Occasionally she will crouch and lean into the music in order to evoke a certain sound from the musicians.

She is almost always praised by music critics not only for her conducting but for performing little-known scores, and her concerts have become musical events to look forward to.

On performance night of *The Pearl Fishers*, Eve waited backstage for curtain time. There were mingled sounds of orchestra members tuning up, singers vocalizing, and the hum of voices from the assembling audience. Eve's daughter Liz, a fourteen-year-old replica of her mother, waited with her. Eve tried to study the score, but she was constantly interrupted by well-wishers—people flocking backstage to say good luck in French, Italian, and English.

Nicolai Gedda came in to wish her luck. "You know," she told him wonderingly, "I'm nervous tonight. I don't understand it. I'm usually never nervous. I think it's because I have no last-minute crisis to attend to." She showed the tenor how she had changed something relating to his aria. "I'm going to hold the note as long as you want me to," she said. "I'll hold it until you turn purple." The two of them laughed and kissed each other.

Eve's husband and her son Andy came backstage to say good luck. Eve looked admiringly at her tall, good-looking son and in a joking, motherly tone said, "Hey, you look nice. What happened?" Then she noticed his scuffed, unpolished shoes and said, "You forgot to change your shoes." Andy assured her that he didn't forget but had chosen to wear them. Later, with a mock sigh, Eve said to a well-wisher, "Did you see the shoes Andy was wearing?"

When Eve began worrying that some friends wouldn't get seats for the evening, her daughter said protectively, "Mother, other people will take care of them. You should sit and relax."

"You're right," Eve responded, "I should relax." She sat down, then got up again. A few minutes later she decided to change from her comfortable shoes to the high-heeled satin shoes that she would wear on stage. Someone came by and asked if she wanted the door closed so she could study. "No, leave the door open," Eve answered. "If anyone needs me, they'll know I'm available."

And then it was time for the concert. As the singers started to file onstage, Eve said laughingly, "Goodbye. I'm not coming with you." A few minutes later, composed and lovely, she was out on stage acknowledging the warm ovation. Then she turned to the orchestra, picked up the baton, and the concert began.

Three months later, on a pleasant afternoon, Eve, wearing pants and a shirt with rolled-up sleeves, her long hair pulled back, stands over the stove in the small kitchen of her New York apartment. She is cooking a pot roast. The table in her large dining room is covered with the music from a score that she and her assistant have been copying all morning. After putting up the pot roast, Eve will coach a soprano for a production of *Traviata* that she is going to conduct in Chattanooga, Tennessee, the following week. When the coaching session is over, she will work on the score for the rest of the day.

Andy is at home during a school vacation. He has been busily shooting baskets through the basketball hoop that hangs in his bedroom. When he was younger, he sang in the children's chorus at the New York City Opera, as did his sister, but gradually his love for sports superseded his musical interest. Although she is too old for the children's chorus, Liz still continues her involvement in music, and there is reason to believe that she will make it her career.

The Quelers have begun to feel cramped in their present apartment and have been trying to move to a new one. They were ready to buy a cooperative apartment but were voted down by the board of directors, who would only take them if Eve agreed not to work with singers in her home—a condition Eve couldn't agree to. Other apartment houses have offered similar restrictions, so for now they must stay where they are.

As Eve browns onions and meat and intermittently munches on a piece of toast, which is her lunch, she talks about the difficulties and joys of a musician's life.

"When I started playing the piano at the age of five," she says, "I had no concept of what a career in music means. My concept was that you play the piano and everybody tells you how good you are. Gradually it became serious, and then it was my whole life. My parents were just as naive. Their idea of a musical career was that I would play the piano in Carnegie Hall. They didn't envision that I would have to travel a lot, would have to go to strange cities, to be alone—that sort of thing. It took them a while to get accustomed to the realities.

"Conducting involves endless studying of scores. In a sense, I'm lucky because I can do a lot of studying in my head and that means I can work on an opera almost any time. I can hear any part of a score at will. If I'm going somewhere on a bus, I decide what I'm going to study and listen to it mentally. If I don't like what I hear, I think it over again, making changes. If I can't hear a piece at will, I know I'm not familiar enough with the music and have to go back and study the score.

"The wonderful thing about conducting is that there is no end to the delving you can do. I don't mean technically anymore. I feel very secure technically. There's always something new to be found in the music. There's always more beauty to be discovered. There's no time when you can say, 'Well, this is it.' You can't re-create a performance. The next one will be different. That one is over, but the next one will always be better. It must be," she adds emphatically.

"There have been really rewarding moments in my years of conducting. For example, during *The Pearl Fishers*, in the first act when Gedda had his aria, he took it very slowly and so beautifully. I wanted the orchestra to be just right for him, but because of where he was standing, I couldn't hear the strings and I didn't know if they were with me or not. He was singing so exquisitely. I didn't want to ruin it. I could only hope the strings were with me. As it turned out, they were, and the aria was such a success.

"One of the most wonderful moments I ever experienced was during the opera *Francesca Da Rimini*, by Zandonai. Placido Domingo and Raina Kabaivanska had a duet. It was so beautiful and so moving that when they were through I couldn't move. The whole orchestra felt that way, and so did the audience." Eve's eyes glow as she talks. "There was so much warmth attached to a moment like that. When something like that happens, the feelings are indescribable. You just know it's worth all the work, all of everything you've put into it."

Eve finishes her cooking and prepares to work with the soprano who has just arrived. When she returns from Chattanooga, there will be more work in New York before going to Barcelona to make her debut in Spain. If Eve feels pressured, she doesn't complain. She is delighted that her career continues to expand. She is clearly a woman who knows the meaning and the joy of work.

Lola Redford

The phone rings in a handsome Fifth Avenue apartment in
New York. A tall, slim, blond woman picks up the receiver
on the third ring and says a pleasant hello into the mouth-
piece.

"May I please speak to Mrs. Redford," asks the voice at
the other end of the line.

"This is Mrs. Redford," answers the young woman.

"Mrs. Robert Redford?" queries the voice.

The woman grimaces, and for a moment her eyes cloud
over. Clearly she is annoyed.

"This is Lola Redford," she says politely but firmly.

The caller accepts the correction without a comment. She
tells Lola Redford that she is the president of a women's
group in New Jersey and she has heard that Lola is one of
the founders of Consumer Action Now (CAN), which has
been an active consumer and environmental lobbying
organization.

"I'm calling," continues the woman, "because I'd like you
to speak to our members on certain aspects of ecology."

"I'd be delighted to," Lola replies. She finds out the date
of the meeting, the amount she will be paid, and agrees to
be there.

"Oh yes, just one more thing," says the woman from New

Jersey. "I hope you don't mind if we tell our members that Robert Redford's wife will be speaking to them."

"Yes, I do mind," Lola answers evenly. "I'm not interested in appearing as a movie star's wife. I'm coming to speak to the group as Lola Redford. My subjects are consumer and environmental problems, not the movies."

"Oh, I understand that. You can talk on whatever you like. We just want our ladies to know that the speaker is a movie star's wife. It will help attendance, you know."

"I'm really not interested in advertising myself as somebody's wife just to help attendance," Lola responds. "If you want a speaker who will do that, you'd better find someone else."

The woman from New Jersey pleads with her to change her mind, but Lola won't be swayed. She has had this conversation before. Not long ago she made up her mind that she wanted to be accepted on her own terms, not as the wife of a famous person. She admits that in past years she did not have the courage to take such a stand and is aware that in the beginning the name Mrs. Robert Redford opened many doors for her. But lately, she has come to realize that she is a person in her own right with an important expertise. She no longer has to trade on anyone else's identity.

Unlike most women who have careers, Lola's early goals had very little to do with pursuing work interests of her own. She entered wholeheartedly into the role of wife and mother, and when her handsome, talented husband achieved fame, she was thrilled and proud to be singled out as Mrs. Robert Redford. Eventually she came to understand that living in someone's reflected glory is not terribly satisfying. So at the age of thirty, when most working women are already well into their professions, Lola Redford began to carve out her career.

Lola, whose maiden name is Van Wagenen, was born in 1938, the oldest of six children. Her birthplace was Provo,

Utah, a town best known for housing Brigham Young University.

"Brigham Young is a very conservative college," comments Lola, "but the university provides a nice atmosphere for the people of the community."

The Van Wagenens were Mormons, as were all their neighbors. Lola explains that orthodox Mormonism is more than just going to church on Sundays. It's a way of behaving with a heavy stress on the importance of the family. There is an emphasis on good health, and Mormons are prohibited from smoking and drinking and are even told what they should eat. As a youngster, Lola was required to belong to a children's organization in which she was taught sewing, cooking, and various outdoor activities—activities deemed necessary for the Mormon woman-to-be.

Lola says she never felt oppressed by the restrictions of her religion and in fact remembers them with pleasure. She points out that the health concerns must be beneficial since Mormons enjoy longevity and have the lowest cancer rate in the country.

Both Lola's parents had a positive influence on her life. "My father is very artistic," she says. "I've always adored the things he does with his hands. He was the president and owner of a radio station when I was a child, but he constantly made things at home that were beautiful—illuminations and manuscripts and that sort of thing. I've inherited his artistic ability and his passion for art."

Lola's mother is an outdoors person—a hiker, a golfer, a tennis player, and a mountain climber. Lola emulates her mother's love of physical activities and excels in many of them. What really pleases Lola is that Mrs. Van Wagenen recently ran for political office in Utah.

"She was the first woman in the county to do it," Lola proudly relates. "She lost, but the fact that she ran is really terrific."

When she was seventeen, Lola was awarded a scholarship to Brigham Young University. "I decided against using it," she confides. "I felt it would be better to get away from home and see how the outside world lived. I had always assumed that gentiles—which is what Mormons call non-Mormons—were a rather peculiar breed, and I was curious to get a look at them."

Lola went to Los Angeles, California, with two friends. The three young women shared an apartment, and Lola went to work in a bank to help pay the rent. To her surprise she found that she had a great deal in common with non-Mormons, that the people she met in Los Angeles were not so different from the folks in Provo, Utah.

"I thought," Lola remembers, "that Mormons had an exclusivity on a certain kind of morality, on a certain kind of behavior. I assumed that loving families were only found among Mormons. I was pleasantly surprised to discover that lots of people liked their families, loved their children, and enjoyed family relationships.

It was during the year in California that Lola met a young art student named Robert Redford. They found they had a great deal in common and became close friends. Very shortly after they met, Robert asked her to marry him.

"I was only eighteen," says Lola, "and although I was crazy about Bob, I thought I was too young to get married."

In order to forget her persistent suitor, the following year Lola returned to Brigham Young for one semester and then popped off to a small college in Hawaii.

"I took such deep subjects as the art of hula dancing and the history of Hawaii," she recalls, smiling. "I wasn't terribly serious and didn't have any concept of preparing myself for a life of work."

Although Lola tends to laugh at her youthful frivolity, she does add that she took a liberal arts curriculum and was very interested in painting and design.

"I always liked to do things with my hands," she explains. "I sewed from the time I was very small, and interior design fascinated me."

If she had any thoughts of fashioning a career for herself, they all vanished when she returned to California after her year in Hawaii and resumed her friendship with Robert Redford. He had not been so easy to forget, and she decided to marry him.

"I always wanted to be independent," says Lola. "That's one of the positive things about being an oldest child. You're given a lot of responsibility at an early age, so you feel a real need to have independence. But when I met Bob, we felt and thought so much alike, and the things we were both interested in were so similar, that it became a matter of joining forces."

The Van Wagenens were very opposed to their oldest daughter marrying at nineteen. They liked her young man, but they viewed him as Bohemian. He was a college drop-out going to art school, and the concerned parents worried about Lola's future. Lola admits that she would feel much the same way if her own daughter wanted to drop out of school and get married at nineteen.

"At first my parents were bothered that Bob wasn't a Mormon," Lola says, "but as time went on, that became less important because my parents came to see that he was a very fine person."

Lola and Bob were married in the Van Wagenens' home in September 1958. Then the newlyweds came to New York and set up housekeeping in a "dumpy" five-flight walkup apartment.

"Bob started art school," Lola recalls, "and I got another job at a bank so we could live. Six months later I was pregnant."

The Redfords' first child, a boy, was born in September 1959. He died suddenly of what is called sudden infant death syndrome in November 1959. The baby's death was devastating to the twenty-year-old mother.

"I couldn't face it for a long time," Lola remembers. "I couldn't talk about it or have anything to do with it. Even after the birth of my other children, it was so painful for me that I had to block it out."

Lola quickly became pregnant again, and a girl, Shauna, was born in November 1960. The Redfords' son, Jamie, was born in May 1962.

Through the 1960s, Lola was totally absorbed with her children. The babies weighed under four pounds at birth and both were afflicted with an illness called hyaline membrane disease.

"The infants had to have blood exchanges," Lola relates. "It wasn't until they were four or five years old that I felt sure they would be all right. I was afraid to leave Shauna with a baby sitter until she was over a year old. I was completely tied down to my house and my kids."

In addition to the constant worry about the children, Lola was involved in another adjustment—being the wife of an aspiring actor. The art student she had married was now determined to make a career in show business, and after Shauna was born, the Redfords moved to California, where Bob began to work in television.

"It wasn't easy being married to an actor," Lola confides. "People in show business become completely wrapped up in what they are doing during their work periods. On the other hand, there are long stretches when they're not doing anything. So either my husband wasn't there at all, or he was constantly around."

The Redfords stayed in California until the summer of 1963. Then Bob decided he wanted to have a home in Utah, and he, Lola, and the two children went there to begin work on it.

"Everyone thought we were absolutely mad to go to Utah," Lola remembers. "At first I thought it was crazy, too. Here I had gotten as far away from my home as possible, only to return with my husband. But now I think it's one of the best things we ever did. It's our home, built with our own hands. We spend summers and holidays there, and the children love it. Bob and I are registered voters in Utah, and we're very involved in the political and ecological life of the state."

In the fall of 1963, Bob left for New York to go into rehearsal for a Broadway play, *Barefoot in the Park*. When the play opened and was an enormous hit, Lola was in Utah with the children.

"One of my big regrets," she says sadly, "is that we didn't have enough money for me to fly to New York for opening night. I missed all the standing up and the bravos. But that's how it was. We had sunk all the money Bob made in television into our house. So I stayed in Utah a little longer, packed up the kids, and drove them back to New York."

The next few years were fairly nomadic ones. The family flew to Europe, where Bob made a film, then off they went to Spain for a respite. "It was the first time," says Lola, "that we had enough money in the bank to relax and enjoy each other and the children."

From Spain, Bob flew to California to make three films in a row, and Lola settled herself, Shauna, and Jamie in an apartment in New York. When Bob had free time between films, Lola went out to the west coast to be with him.

By the time Shauna was in kindergarten and Jamie was in nursery school, Lola was in her late twenties.

"Suddenly," she recalls, "I thought, 'Hey, wait a minute, I should be doing something for myself. I should be using my energy and should be trying to grow somehow.' " Drawing on her artistic ability, she began to do some interior decorating for friends.

"I found that although I enjoyed the work," she relates, "it simply wasn't enough. I wanted to do something to improve the things I cared about. I had become more and more concerned about the problems of the environment, partially because I could see how it was being hurt in Utah and partly because I had decided to raise my children in New York and I was deeply worried about the healthfulness of the environment they were growing up in."

In 1968 Lola met Ilene Goldman, wife of William Goldman, the writer of *Butch Cassidy and the Sundance Kid.* Ilene was from Texas, and like Lola, had a feeling for the land and an interest in conservation.

"For about a year and a half Ilene and I discussed what we could do about ecological problems," Lola relates. "Finally we decided to join a group that was working on saving the environment. We found we couldn't be as active as we wanted to be in someone else's organization, so we got together a few women and had a series of lectures—people came to talk to us on various aspects of ecology. At last it became clear that if we were to be effective, we would have to start our own organization, write up a paper, and disseminate information."

In March 1970, she and Ilene founded Consumer Action Now, an environmental consumer organization, and in October of the same year, Lola took time out to give birth to a healthy daughter, Amy.

The purpose of CAN was to alert people to how they could better handle ecology in their everyday lives. The volunteer members rented a two-room office and began to put out a newsletter containing information about the environment. Later they expanded their research to include consumer problems. Money from subscriptions to the newsletter paid the rent for the office.

Lola did research and wrote articles on a variety of subjects: the slaughter of the American buffalo; pesticides; the decline of the osprey, a hawk that feeds on fish; the Marine Mammal Protection Act; and no-fault insurance.

Other women in CAN were telling readers about types of packaging to avoid in supermarkets and what legislation they should support that would help the environment. Every time the group came up with new important information, they would go off to Washington to lobby for it. They were also urging readers of their newsletter to vote for legislators who had conservationist ideas.

Lola, who had functioned primarily as wife and mother for ten years, was now meeting with the legislative director of the Federal Environmental Protection Agency and corresponding with prize-winning, ecology minded scientists. In 1973 her major concern was no-fault insurance, and on January 23, 1974, her CAN article on the subject was placed in the Congressional Record by Sen. Frank E. Moss.

As CAN began to grow in reputation, the two organizers, Ilene and Lola, were in demand as speakers and as guest panelists on local and national television talk shows.

"I must say," Lola confides, "that doing the national shows was enough to traumatize me forever. To hear that music that you've always heard and to know that you're on next and that you have to talk about the environment is absolutely a stunning experience. Just before I went on the "Dick Cavett Show" I thought, 'What am I doing here?' I called Bob and said, 'Hey, I'm really nervous. This is something that I wanted to do and now that I'm here, I'm scared. What shall I do?' And he gave me a terrific piece of advice. He said, 'Go on and just listen to him talk. Don't think about anything. Whatever he says, just respond to him.' It worked. It went terrifically well. From the "Dick Cavett Show" alone we received 7,000 letters, and subscriptions to our newsletter went from 200 to 5,000 in six months."

Lola concedes that not all television appearances were quite so successful. She shudders as she remembers her appearance with Ilene on the "David Frost Show."

"It was a complete disaster," Lola relates. "We had expected it to be wonderful. We had a preshow interview with a woman who asked us the five most important questions David Frost could ask us. We thought, 'How terrific.' But when the show started, we got the message it wasn't going to work. He introduced us as Mrs. Robert Redford and Mrs. William Goldman, and we knew we weren't going to be taken seriously. We weren't. He asked us questions like, 'What would you say was the silliest product you've ever run into?' To top it all off, during a station break he turned to Ilene and me and said, 'Don't you understand that you're boring my audience?' " Lola breaks into gales of laughter at the memory. "I didn't know whether to laugh or to get up and leave. We stayed and finished the show, but it was awful. The incredible thing was, when we were getting ready to go, he came over to kiss us good-bye." Lola laughs again. "I think we got about three letters from that show."

In the early days of CAN Lola and Ilene were the only ones in demand for speaking engagements, but as the group has gained recognition, people are willing to accept other CAN members as speakers. This pleases Lola, who views CAN as a totally democratic organization and doesn't like the concept of some members having more prestige than others. She admits that she and Ilene function in an executive capacity but only in the sense that they make decisions and see that certains things are followed through.

"It's also our responsibility to look ahead and see where

things are going," Lola explains. "We are the ones who go out and sell ideas."

Lola has been instrumental in selling a book to Ballantine Books written by members of CAN. The book includes interviews with young people giving their views on how they think the world will be in twenty years and how parents can prepare their children for the future changes.

When Betty Furness went on NBC news with her consumer program, Lola and Ilene asked to have CAN do research for her and to submit ideas they considered important. Their request was granted, and many of CAN's ideas were used.

In 1974 CAN created a filmstrip on litter, narrated by Robert Redford, to be shown in schools. On a summer afternoon the women held a screening for the children of CAN members. The boys and girls filed into the comfortably furnished CAN office and sat cross-legged on the floor. The children laughed and applauded the cartoon characters on the screen. Afterwards they were shown a large box that contained various empty food packages. One of the women described to the children how they could make toys out of the packages rather than making garbage out of them.

Lola explained to a visitor that this was all part of an environmental campaign that CAN planned to wage in the schools. Her eyes shone as she outlined the endless ways of reaching people of all ages. She is justifiably proud of this grass-roots organizaiton, which she helped to found.

Lola Redford greets an early morning visitor to her New York apartment dressed in blue jeans and a beige turtleneck sweater. Her face is scrubbed clean and her blond hair is pulled tightly back in a ponytail.

The Redfords's ten-room apartment, which occupies the

entire floor of a large apartment house, has been tastefully decorated by Lola. The spacious living room, with its enormous brick fireplace and its view of Central Park, is done in rich browns and white. It has an easy, lived-in look. Large potted plants sit at well-lighted windows, and the room abounds with handsome paintings. Two of the pictures have American Indian motifs. The Redfords brought them for the Utah house but liked them so much that they brought them back to New York.

Lola sits on one of the comfortable brown couches in front of the fireplace and rests her coffee cup on the huge glass coffee table, which she designed.

I still love doing interior decoration," Lola comments, looking with satisfaction at her handiwork. "I like doing it for my friends, but I wouldn't want to do it professionally.

"Working for CAN has really been wonderful for me, and I will be involved in this work for a long time," she continues. "It's a good organization because it can be flexible and grow.

"The relationship with the women in CAN has perhaps been as satisfying as the work itself. It has been the antithesis of everything you've ever heard about women. They don't feel competitive with each other. They are willing to listen and exchange ideas. These women will be friends of mine for the rest of my life.

"Because of my work with CAN my life has changed on a very practical level. My buying habits have changed. I have gotten away from prepackaged anything—no frozen dinners, no frozen soufflés, no white bread, no paper napkins or paper towels. I became a label-reader, which I had never was before. Then I wanted to know what those labels meant. I became more concerned with everything I brought into the house. Since New York doesn't have many recycling centers, I felt we had to give up things that ordinarily you would recycle. So we've stopped buying drinks that are put in aluminum cans. I'm not totally rigid on this. I do break down and get the kids a can of soda from time to time. One thing we've tried to do is not make caring for the ecology a burden.

"I think the children are pleased that I work, and they often ask me questions about what CAN is doing. They're especially interested in the book we're writing because we are interviewing teen-agers, and they want to hear the responses from the kids. The only times the children resent my work is when I'm away.

"When you have a dad who is famous, it's probably nice to see that your mother doesn't feel overwhelmed by the fame. The children have to face living with a father who is well-known, and when they see that it doesn't stop me from doing something, I suspect it gives them a confidence about doing something on their own.

"Although I don't get paid for working with CAN—whatever we make on lectures goes back into the organization—I do like the idea of earning my own money. When I think of the book we're doing, I think how nice it would be if we made money on it and each of the women could have some money of her own. There's a sense of pride in earning your own way. It's been a long time since I've done that. Although it's not necessary for the upkeep of my household, there's something freeing psychologically about it. You know that if anything happens you can take care of yourself.

"Having my own life has made it easier for my husband. He's relieved of the responsibility of having to create an ego for me. He knows that the things I'm doing are making me very happy and I don't have to rely on the things he will bring me.

"We should all have something of our own," Lola concludes. "We should have something of our own because we're all here alone. That's one of the things I learned by losing a child—that you really have to go through the traumas of life by yourself. No one, even when you're married and have children, is going to help you when it gets down to that final crunch. No one can. It's what you're made of that's going to make whatever experience you run into either a positive experience for you or something that takes you down. To be able to rely on oneself in all sorts of circumstances and to put yourself in a position where you can test things out are both very good and positive."

Marlene Sanders

ABC-TV producer Marlene Sanders enters the editing room at the television studios, glances at the floor, which is covered with masses of tangled film, and says quite calmly, "What a mess!" She then pulls up a stool to begin the important work of editing her one-hour documentary show about the television industry.

Dressed in a pants suit and wearing horn-rimmed glasses, the attractive producer takes out her stopwatch and discusses some of the problems of the show with the film editor.

The editor starts the film, and the documentary, which has been four months in the making, appears on the small editing room screen. A shot of Marlene, who does some of the interviewing in the show, comes on. "Hey," she says happily in her no-nonsense voice, "you got rid of that ugly cutaway of me." An interviewee appears, his speech interspersed with many "ah, ah, ahs." Marlene listens to him in despair. "Such a nice guy," she says, "but such a bumbler." She has the section played back and groans as she hears it again. Finally a way is worked out to get rid of the stammering. They will superimpose some pictures over his talking, then when the "ahs" are cut, there won't be a problem with lip synchronization.

A few minutes later Marlene emphatically crosses out large sections in the manuscript, then laughs. "I have just struck out the president of ABC," she says. "I think he'll be glad when he sees the sequence."

Back in her simple, modern office with its standard desk and file cabinets, Marlene settles down to do more work on the script. On one of the office walls are pictures of the producer in action—on location and interviewing people. There are several framed awards including a special citation from NOW (National Organization for Women) for a show called "The Hand That Rocks The Ballot Box." The inscription reads, "AN OUTSTANDING PROGRAM DOCUMENTING THE EMERGENCE OF WOMEN AS A POLITICAL POWER."

Marlene apologizes to a visitor for the lack of interior decoration in her office. "I've spent so much time around newsrooms," she explains, "that I don't pay much attention to surroundings."

What she neglects to say is that her continual involvement in her work doesn't leave her much time for or interest in frivolities, whether they be furnishings, clothes, or cosmetics. It is probably this single-mindedness and concentration that has enabled Marlene Sanders to rise slowly, step by step, in the male-dominated world of broadcasting, from a seventy-five-dollar-a-week assistant to the producer on a local television station, to a highly paid, autonomous producer for a major network.

Marlene was born January 10, 1931, in Cleveland, Ohio. When she was a year old her parents were divorced and her father left Cleveland to live in Philadelphia. By the time she was three and a half, both parents had remarried. Marlene continued to live with her mother and stepfather and, eventually, a half-brother eight years her junior, and vacations and summers were with her father, stepmother, and twin half-brothers.

Marlene recalls, "I sort of shuffled back and forth

between my two families. Some kids are born with silver spoons in their mouths. I was born carrying a suitcase."

The traveling was fun for her, although she disliked it when her mother invariably sat her next to some elderly woman who was asked to keep an eye on the little girl. "The women always bored me," Marlene remembers. "I was kind of a loner, and as I got older I'd figure out ways to avoid all those kindly strangers."

Neither of Marlene's parents had any notion that their pretty, blue-eyed daughter would grow up to have a career. Of her father she says, "His influence on my life was really negligible. What I got from him were inherited things—his sort of sour, mean streak, and, I hope, his intelligence."

She feels the key relationship in her life was the one with her mother, although even today she views it as exceedingly complicated. "My mother and I look very much alike, but that's where the similarity stops," observes Marlene. "Two more different people you could never meet. My mother is sort of giddy and gossipy and highly competitive— competitive in how people look and how they react to her. She's very good-looking, and appearances are terribly important to her."

Marlene doesn't remember exactly when she became aware of these qualities in her mother—qualities so opposite from her own down-to-earth personality. As a young girl in elementary school, Marlene became intensely interested in theater and starred in all the school plays. "That was fine with my mother," she recalls. "It was acceptable and reflected well on her. But later, when I hit adolescence, we got along miserably. It was really stormy—very bad for both of us. I would come home from a date and she would want to hear all about it. What did somebody wear? What did they serve? Were the parents there?" Marlene screws up her face in disgust at the memory. "I would never say anything about all that. I couldn't stand to talk about it. We used to have really screaming battles. It was terrible. She really rubbed me the wrong way," she recalls, "although in many ways we were very close."

Marlene's mother was upwardly mobile, and the family was always moving into better and better neighborhoods. "My mother wanted us to be with the right people," relates Marlene, "and, to her credit, to go to the best schools."

When Marlene was in the ninth grade, the family moved to Shaker Heights, the wealthiest section of Cleveland, with an excellent school. Marlene remembers how she suddenly became aware that her family had less money than their neighbors. "I saw that all my friends wore cashmere sweaters, belonged to country clubs, and lived in mansions. Our house was nice, but it certainly wasn't a mansion. The kids went bowling after school and that was expensive. I could never afford to go with them."

Since she couldn't compete financially, she made it her business to compete scholastically and theatrically. She pushed herself hard to get good grades—"except in Latin and math where I was totally hopeless"—became a big wheel on the school radio station, and appeared in most of the school plays. "I was going to be a great actress, a big star. On all my yearbooks everybody wrote, 'We'll see you on Broadway,' and that sort of thing." Marlene laughs, embarrassed by the recollection.

During her high school years Marlene became interested in left-wing politics—an interest that set her apart from the conservative Shaker Heights community but played an important part in her career years later. During the 1948 presidential campaign, she was the only one in her neighborhood who wore a button supporting the Progressive party candidate, Henry Wallace.

Marlene knew, when she graduated high school, that her family could only afford one year of college. She went to Ohio State for the allotted time and then, filled with ambition—"I was eighteen and I thought if I'm not a success as an actress by the time I'm twenty-one, I'm a has-been"—she went back to Cleveland and apprenticed at the Cleveland Playhouse for one year.

"I guess it was during that year," relates Marlene, "that I began to get the drift of things, that I really wasn't going to make it as an actress. I was getting the idea that I wasn't that good. I still wouldn't admit it, but I just knew it. Also I was pretty fat. I always had a weight problem, and my weight was continually up and down. At that time I was up."

When her year at the playhouse was over, Marlene did secretarial work and research in the political science department at Western Reserve University. "A very bad year," she remembers. Overriding her misgivings about her talents as an actress, she applied to the Hedgerow Theatre in Philadelphia to work under the well-known director Jasper Deeter and was accepted.

"I think my mother was very upset with what I was doing," says Marlene. "She wanted me to get married. I was going with a very nice guy, Buddy Kahn, on and off for a long time, and during my year at Hedgerow we kept in touch. When I finished at Hedgerow I was twenty-one and I knew I had had it as an actress. I decided to marry Buddy."

In May of her twenty-first year, to the delight of her mother, Marlene became the bride of tall, handsome Samuel Kahn. After a summer in Cleveland, the young couple moved to New York, where Buddy enrolled in Columbia Teacher's College to become a psychologist and Marlene took a series of jobs while pursuing a theatrical career.

"I still have my W2 forms from that year," she says. "I had twenty-one jobs. I typed and taught swimming—I guess I mostly typed—and I had a few off-Broadway jobs. I was also making the Broadway rounds with other aspiring actresses."

Two summers after coming to New York, Marlene's acting career was still uneventful. Deciding to try something different, she took a job as an assistant to the producer at a summer theatre in Matunuck, Rhode Island, called the Theatre By The Sea. It never occurred to Marlene, as she packed to go to Rhode Island, that her summer stint would prove to be a crucial turning point in her life.

The Theatre By The Sea was not only a theater but an inn and restaurant as well. Twenty-four-year-old Marlene did everything: read scripts, paid the waiters' salaries, found lodgings for actors, and any other chore that no one else wanted to do.

Buddy worked in a mental hospital that summer, and husband and wife saw each other on weekends. Their marriage, shaky from the very beginning, was definitely falling apart. It was increasingly clear to both of them that they were friends and not much more. They decided to get a divorce at the end of the summer.

In her job, Marlene was meeting vast numbers of people who were involved in theater and television. To anyone who might be able to help her, she mentioned that she was looking for a position for the fall. One young man, named Mike Wallace, told her that he was starting a new TV news show on a local New York network. He promised to introduce her to the producer, who was looking for an assistant.

In the fall of 1955 Marlene started a new life. She was hired by television producer Ted Yates, she moved into her own apartment, filed for a divorce from Buddy, and began going to a psychotherapist. "I went into therapy," she explains, "because I had screwed things up in my marriage and I thought I should get some kind of help. I went twice a week for almost three years. The therapist encouraged me to examine certain behavior patterns, and I think it was beneficial."

Professionally her life had certainly taken a turn for the better. Ted Yates was a producer whose career was on the upswing, and Marlene went along with him, learning the ins and outs of the television business. She was the production assistant on the seven and eleven o'clock news, and her job was to sort the scripts, get the artwork, pick the music, and edit the film.

"Ted Yates was a great guy," Marlene recalls. "He would give you all the responsibility you could handle. He told me to do things and I did them. What did I know about editing film? I didn't know anything. But I learned. It was a great opportunity."

Although her salary at the time was seventy-five dollars a week, she most often took home ninety dollars because of extensive overtime. "I never felt so well off in my whole life as I did in those days," Marlene remembers. "I had my own apartment and I was even able to send money to my brother at the Massachusetts Institute of Technology." She laughs. "I was rich."

After a year Marlene became associate producer of the Mike Wallace interview show, "Night Beat." She booked the guests and began to see how the scripts were constructed. Wallace, a very forthright interviewer, was at the height of his popularity, and the show was an exciting one to be involved with. Marlene worked, uncomplainingly, until midnight every night. She was also branching out—writing a few programs on the side, including a sports show for tennis star Gussie Moran.

In 1957 Mike Wallace left the local network and went to ABC. He was replaced by John Wingate, and Marlene was promoted to coproducer. However, with Wallace gone, "Night Beat" was losing its high rating, and Marlene, seeing the end of the show in sight, began to write some half-hour documentaries. Her professional life was expanding, as was her personal life; she met her future husband, Jerry Toobin.

Jerry was manager of Symphony of the Air, an orchestra composed of former members of the NBC Symphony Orchestra under the baton of veteran conductor Leopold Stokowski. Marlene had booked Stokowski as a guest on "Night Beat," and when he backed out at the last minute, Jerry's secretary called and suggested that her boss, Jerry Toobin, appear instead. After reading his biography, Marlene told the secretary that Mr. Toobin sounded interesting but they would prefer a member of the orchestra rather than the manager.

Subsequently Marlene and Jerry talked on the phone several times. Jerry was an ardent viewer of "Night Beat" and had seen Marlene's name on the screen for years. Some writers on "Night Beat," who had met Jerry, told Marlene he was a nice guy and she ought to get to know him. When he invited her to a concert she was delighted to accept.

The tall, silver-haired man in his late thirties, and the blue-eyed, red-haired, twenty-seven-year-old woman were immediately drawn to each other. They were both tremendously ambitious, shared a deep interest in politics and music, and had respect for each other's talents. Three weeks after their first date, they decided to get married. "We were able to decide so quickly," explains Marlene, "because we both had been married before and we had fairly certain ideas of exactly what we wanted." The wedding took place on May 27, 1958.

Toward the end of 1959 Marlene was pregnant, and her job was coming to an end. She decided to quit when the baby was born. "I wasn't thinking of doing it permanently," she says, "but summer is a slow time for TV and I knew I wanted to look for a new position."

The Toobins' son, Jeffrey, was born in May 1960. He was

an easy, amiable baby and by August of the same year Marlene was ready to go back to work. "At that time," she remembers, "Jerry's salary was pretty low. We could manage on what he earned, but just barely. However, that wasn't the motivating factor for my working. I was still going to make my own mark. Jerry was never anything but enthusiastic about that. He has always been a great booster of mine. I was the best." Marlene laughs embarrassedly. "He still says that I'm the best. I think he's crazy but he seems to mean it. It's very nice because he's so encouraging. We're both very competitive people, but I don't think we ever compete against each other."

Marlene's first job after Jeffrey was born was handling a radio and TV public relations show for the Arthritis Foundation. After three months she went to Westinghouse Broadcasting for a year and a half, where she produced a show called "P.M." From Westinghouse she was hired by a local New York radio station, WNEW, as assistant to the news director. For two and a half years Marlene produced weekly radio documentaries, writing them and editing all the tapes. In addition, she ran a news workshop with students from several universities. Because of a newspaper strike, she even did some broadcasting.

"Just as I was feeling really overworked," recalls Marlene, "I read that ABC-TV was looking for another correspondent. I thought, 'What the hell. I'll give it a try.' I auditioned and I was hired."

With her usual knack for being in the right place at the right time, Marlene went to ABC just before a slight upheaval occurred at the network, an event that would serve to elevate her career another notch. It was during a New York senatorial election year and Lisa Howard, ABC anchorperson for the afternoon news show, came out in support of Senator Keating, who was being opposed by Robert Kennedy. The policy at ABC was that news people

not express their own political opinions, and Lisa Howard
was suspended. Marlene was given her job. Says Marlene,
"Three weeks at ABC and I was thrown into anchoring the
afternoon news. At first it was on a temporary basis, but
three months later the show was permanently mine."

Perhaps because of her early theater training, Marlene
was always self-possessed on camera. "I did have to remind
myself to smile and be a little loose," she remembers. "My
feeling was that women had to be very matter-of-fact and
businesslike on the air to eradicate the image of the flighty
nitwit. Today I don't think that's a consideration, but at the
time I felt it was."

Having her own news show added another dimension to
Marlene's life. ABC was constantly sending their anchor
people where the big stories were, and she found herself
traveling to various parts of the country where anything
newsworthy was happening. In 1964, during the presidential election campaign, she was with Lady Bird Johnson,
wife of Lyndon B. Johnson, on a whistle-stop trip through
the south. Later, she accompanied presidential hopeful
Eugene McCarthy and ultimately was at the White House
reporting on President Johnson's inauguration and on
Lynda Bird Johnson's wedding.

Her most memorable assignment was in war-torn Viet-
name in 1966. "I hadn't requested to be sent there," recalls
Marlene. "My boss asked me if I would go and then said,
'Don't tell me right now. Think about it and let me know.'
Of course, right away I knew I would go, but I thought,
'Well, I'll go home and talk it over.' Jerry said, 'Great!
Fantastic opportunity!' So I went and stayed a month."

Marlene remembers feeling frightened before leaving for
Vietnam but losing her fear once she arrived and started to
work. Although she wasn't in the combat zone—"I didn't
go to Vietnam to prove I wasn't afraid"—she traveled to
Saigon, Danang, and Pleiku observing living conditions and

filming the wounded in hospitals. She was sending film and commentary back to the United States daily. Unexpectedly, there were large Buddhist demonstrations protesting the South Vietnam government which Marlene was able to witness and film. Although she wasn't where the actual fighting was, Marlene remembers that there was always danger. "You could get killed by just riding down the road in a jeep," she says.

The experience in Vietnam was fascinating and upsetting. Marlene had not been prepared for the incredible poverty of the people and the enormous suffering of the war victims. She came back to the United States deeply distressed by her country's involvement in the destruction of the small, beautiful country of Vietnam.

In 1964, while anchoring her afternoon show for ABC, Marlene achieved a first for a woman in news. she anchored the evening news. An anchorperson for the seven o'clock and the eleven o'clock news fell ill and Marlene was chosen to replace him. "It was such a success," she says sarcastically, "that I had to wait seven years until 1971 before I was asked to do it again. However, second time round I did it for three months." It wasn't that her initial try hadn't been successful. It was simply that ABC was reluctant to admit a woman into the male world of evening news. As short as her stint was as evening anchorperson, it did break the ice for women.

In August 1966, Marlene became pregnant for the second time, and she and Jerry looked forward to being the parents of two children. The baby, a boy, was born prematurely in February 1968 and was severely retarded. Marlene saw the baby in the hospital, and then Jerry took him to a home for retarded children. It was a year before she could bring herself to visit her second son.

"It was very rough," she says, "and very hard for me to come to terms with. Everything had been going so well, and when my second child was born, I realized that you can't count on life. The experience really made me humble—made me aware that I shouldn't ever get too smug about things."

Today she visits the child regularly because she feels she should, but it's difficult, since the youngster doesn't seem to have any remembrance of her from one visit to the next.

A year and a half after Marlene's return from Vietnam, there was an economic crisis at ABC and the news department was forced to drop several shows. Marlene's afternoon show was one of the casualties. She became a full-time correspondent on the evening news which meant that she had to travel a great deal in order to get stories.

"It was a period of my life when I was never able to plan anything," she relates. "I'd go away for two or three days at a time. Once the news desk sent me down to West Virginia to cover a mine disaster. I was gone eight days. I enjoyed it up to a point, but after a while I got tired of being shuffled around."

Another factor that made Marlene's life less than perfect was the periodic change of producers for the news show. "Producers have favorites among the correspondents," comments Marlene, "and if you're a favorite, you're on the air a great deal. If you're out of favor, you don't get good stories and you're not on. Sometimes you would be a favorite with a producer for a while and then he would lose interest in you. I shared offices with other correspondents, and you would see them rise and fall. It made me feel shaky."

She saw that being a woman worked against her—the good stories invariably went to men. Longing to have more challenging assignments, Marlene began to take leaves from the correspondents category to produce documentaries. No other correspondent was doing anything like that.

In 1970, Marlene produced two half-hour documentaries. One, called "Women's Liberation," was the first show on network television about the women's movement. The other, titled "We Have Met the Enemy and He Is Us," dealt with overpopulation. "Strangers in Their Own Land—The Blacks" was Marlene's contribution to a three-program ABC news study of minority groups in America. "Children in Peril," in 1972, was a hard look at child abuse.

As a full-time producer in January 1973, Marlene produced her first one-hour documentary, "Population—Boom or Doom," based on the Commission of Population Growth Report. "I was apprehensive about doing a commission report as a show," she recalls. "How do you make a report dramatically interesting? It was hard work, but the show came out well."

The critics agreed. John O'Connor of the *New York Times* wrote, "Produced and written by Marlene Sanders, the hour-long study of the presidential report is solid, fair, unafraid . . . unsensational, but steadily absorbing."

Marlene's second hour documentary was shown in September 1973. Again its theme was women's liberation and was called "Woman's Place." John Voorhees of the *Seattle Times* commented in his enthusiastic review ". . . an important effort and one which deserves to be seen by men."

It is not a coincidence that Marlene produced two documentaries dealing with the women's movement. She was one of its earliest enthusiasts. During the days of her afternoon show she became a charter member of the National Organization for Women and frequently lectured on women's rights. In 1972 she joined a women's group at ABC that was dedicated to improving the position of women at the network. The group has become very successful and a strong affirmative action program ensuring fair hiring practices now exists at ABC. "Employment of women has increased in every category," relates Marlene. "I feel that my show, 'Woman's Place,' was done in part because of the pressures on management from our group."

The most difficult show, emotionally, that Marlene produced between 1970 and 1974 was her January 1974 documentary "The Right To Die," in which she explored the generally taboo subject of death. Part of the show was devoted to psychiatrists and doctors interviewing people who were terminally ill. It was a painful experience for Marlene and her staff. While filming the show, they were forced to confront their own fears of death. Marlene became obsessed with the subject, even to the point of dreaming about it.

"It upset me to film the interviews with all those people," she recalls. "I worried that the lights were too hot for them and I kept thinking we were invading their privacy. But they didn't mind. In fact they seemed glad to be able to talk, and they enjoyed seeing themselves on television."

Despite the fact that many television viewers preferred not to watch a show about death, and even though there was no sponsor for the documentary, "The Right To Die" was a successful show and received glowing reviews. Wrote Alan M. Kriegsman of the *Washington Post*, "This isn't the easiest program to watch, but it does repay the attentive viewer with far more than the usual prime-time rewards."

As soon as the show was finished, Marlene, who is rarely ill and seldom sees a doctor, went immediately for a complete physical checkup.

When Marlene is not working at ABC, she relaxes at home in her spacious, modern apartment. The Toobins are unpretentious people, and their simple, comfortable furnishings reflect this. Some walls are lined with neatly catalogued books, while others feature paintings, including one that Marlene brought back from Vietnam. In the hallway are framed awards and pictures of Marlene with various celebrities: Richard Nixon, Patricia Nixon, and Sophia

Loren. There are pictures of Jerry, now a producer with public television, and some of Jeffrey. A lovely watercolor was a present from Lyndon and Lady Bird Johnson.

Tonight Jerry and Jeffrey are away. Marlene eats a dieter's supper and talks about her work and the role of women in broadcasting.

"When you produce a show," she relates, "you can make an analogy to a painter with a blank canvas. You have an idea and you have to execute it. With film, you have to come up with a plan, then find ways of executing it. You organize it, you do administrative work—get a film crew, worry about budget, worry about staff. You're concerned with who will do the interviews—will it be you or somebody else? You have to set it all up and find the right people to interview. That's very difficult. Sometimes the right people don't want to talk to you. When you've done the groundwork, then you shoot it and edit it.

"I always write my own show. I couldn't stand to have it any other way. Only I know the research I did before I even shot a foot of film, so how could anybody else write it?"

"My most favorite show is always the one I'm working on. I become very involved with each documentary. I think about it all the time. I go swimming once a week and I think about it while I'm swimming laps. I do some of my best thinking while I'm swimming." Marlene laughs. "I have to be careful that I don't become a bore at home. Everybody gets sick of hearing me talk so much about a certain subject.

"I'm always concerned about my future. I wonder if I want to go on producing indefinitely or do I want to go into management. The thing about this business is that it's pointless to think about it. So many things have happened because somebody has offered me something. Something comes up. Circumstances change. The guy you're working for, who considers you the greatest, gets fired. He leaves and an enemy comes in. A colleague goes to a large network and gets a big job and asks you to come over in another capacity. I turned down a big job at NBC in local news. I like what I'm doing now. I enjoy having the amount of control I have. It's more satisfying than just being part of putting together an amorphous news show.

"I've tried to have a perspective on my career. When I was on camera every day with my afternoon show, and at the height of the publicity about me, I don't think I ever kidded myself that I was a star. Never. These things are shifty. They're dependent on a lot of different things. You just can't take it too seriously. I have learned that there are several things important about my work: number one, how I feel about it; number two, how my colleagues in the profession feel about it. There was a time in my life when what people thought was more important to me. After a while I didn't have to impress anyone. It didn't matter what the audience thought or whether there were clippings in the hometown paper. Obviously I want to do good work and I want to be recognized for it, but I would rather have the recognition from people in the business. I have no interest in being recognized on the street or in the supermarket.

"I'm glad that my success has opened doors for other women in broadcasting. Since I anchored the evening news, other women have done it. Still, no women are anchoring the evening news regularly. I think it will be a long time before women will have an equal place in broadcasting with men. It will only come when women are accepted as authority figures. The anchorman of the evening is papa. There's still too much hostility toward women or lack of respect for them. It has to do with society. Television is a follower, not a leader. Until it's damn safe to do it, they won't do it."

Marlene looks up from her Spartan supper with her direct, intelligent gaze. It is quite clear that she will never be a follower.

Gertrude Schimmel

The gray-haired woman in a plaid shirtwaist dress picks up the phone. "Hi Sam," she says in a crisp, New York-accented, nasal voice. "Listen, there's a reporter here and he feels mortified because he forgot a morning appointment." The hard pronunciation of her *d*'s and *t*'s marks her as Bronx born and raised. "He wants to apologize, so be nice to him," she urges the man at the other end of the line. Then Inspector Gertrude Schimmel of the New York Police Department hangs up the phone and laughs with gusto. The lines around her brown eyes crinkle up, and her unmadeup face glows rosy red.

"That poor reporter is a wreck," she says with compassion, "but I think everything will be all right."

And it probably will be, for Inspector Schimmel is a police officer whose words carry considerable weight. After more than thirty years on the force she is the highest-ranking policewoman in the city of New York, and very likely in the country. Now an inspector in charge of public information, she is the first woman in the department to have been promoted to the rank of captain.

When other cops talk about her, it's usually with wonder and respect. "She sure is an unusual woman," is a frequent comment and is often accompanied by an unbelieving shake of the head.

She is scrupulously honest, enormously intelligent, totally lacking in pretension, considerate of the people she deals with, a fighter for what she believes in, and a devoted wife and mother. She is, indeed, a very unusual woman.

Gertrude Schimmel was born in the Bronx, New York, on December 9, 1918, the youngest of three children. Her father and mother, Asher and Ida Tannenbaum, were immigrants who left Austria shortly after the turn of the century. Asher first worked in a clothing factory and later had a small egg business. Ida took care of the home and raised her son and two daughters. She died when Gertrude was sixteen, at which time the youngest daughter assumed the household responsibilities.

Gertrude recalls a financially poor but emotionally rich homelife. As the youngest she was the family pet and could tag along with her mother.

"I was kind of a bright, all-around girl, I guess," relates Gertrude. "I played in the streets with the other kids and I was pretty athletic. I started playing tennis when I was twelve."

She was also an excellent student, winning a state scholarship upon graduation from high school and making Phi Beta Kappa at Hunter College in New York City.

In college Gertrude's goal was to become a high school English teacher. "That was during the depression, when work was scarce," she remembers. "We were told at Hunter that no exams were being given for teachers and we should look around for other jobs."

Available positions seemed to be in civil service, and the juniors and seniors at Hunter took every exam that was offered, including the policewoman's examination.

"At first," she explains, "it was just another exam. Then it began to sound good. It was a great salary. Next to teaching it was the highest salary you could get. I also thought that it would probably offer a lot more variety than teaching. I was right."

There were twenty vacancies for policewomen and 3,700 women applied. When the list came out in 1939, Gertrude had placed third on the exams. Since she was only twenty, she had to wait a year before she became twenty-one and was eligible for appointment to the department.

When Asher Tannenbaum heard that his daughter was going to become a policewoman, he expressed his disapproval. "I thought he was against it because he felt it was dangerous or something like that," reminisces Gertrude. "Later he said he was against it because he thought if I liked the career so much I wouldn't want to get married." She laughs heartily. "I was a kind of independent minded kid, though, I was gonna do what I wanted to do."

Asher Tannenbaum need not have worried about Gertrude's interest in marriage. She became a bride just three months after she joined the Police Department.

While waiting to enter the Police Academy, Gertrude worked at a state civil service job—"It came from one of the exams I took." She was also enjoying an active social life. A pretty, vivacious, dark-haired young woman, she had many dates, so it was no surprise to her when her girl friend's boyfriend said he wanted to introduce her to his good friend Alfred Schimmel. Alfred, he told her, worked as a clerk in the city tax department. Gertrude agreed to the introduction and a double date was arranged for the ballet.

"I had other boyfriends," Gertrude explains. "So as far as I was concerned this was just another date. I was at my girl friend's house the evening we were to go to the ballet and the two men came in with a third friend. The third friend happened to be a magnificent looking, tall blond. I had jet black hair and I always liked blond boys, but I never had a blond boyfriend for some reason. So when this blond guy came in I thought he was my date. But no, it was the dark one who was my date. The blond one came as a chauffeur. It was his car we were going in."

Alfred was very taken with Gertrude that first evening, while she claims that she was neutral about him. "I had a very active social life, so I wasn't in need of a boyfriend," she explains.

After the date Alfred's friend told Gertrude that Alfred wanted to buy a series of theater tickets and wondered if she would go with him.

"I said, 'Yeah, if he buys them I'll go with him. What do I care.' But after the first month, I really liked him."

On June 5, 1940, twenty-one-year-old Gertrude Tannenbaum entered the Police Department, and on September 13 she was married to Alfred Schimmel. "I met my husband on January 13 and we said we'd get married on the thirteenth. We thought it was our lucky number."

Alfred understood from the start that his wife was intent on a career. "He was a very modern man for those days," Gertrude remarks. "He said he wouldn't marry a woman who didn't want a career. He felt that women who stayed home were kind of parasites. He and all his friends were that way. I, for my part, wouldn't have married a man who felt differently. My husband and I worked at jobs and shared the work at home. When the kids came, we both took care of them."

At the police academy Gertrude received classroom and physical training. She recalls that the men and women were identically trained, except that the women were excluded from the daily one-mile run and from boxing.

One day, while in class at the academy, Gertrude was called from the room and sent downtown to the office of the director of policewomen. "Of course, all the way downtown I was scared," she remembers. "I didn't know what I had done wrong."

At the office, Gertrude was told there was a special job

for her. She was to go to a precinct in Brooklyn to meet two detectives. When she arrived she would learn the details of her assignment.

"I wanted to ask why they had selected me," she confides, "but I didn't. Later I learned they had asked for someone of a certain height and coloring and I fit the bill."

In Brooklyn the detectives told Gertrude that a threatening note had been delivered to a local merchant advising him his daughter would be killed unless she placed a certain amount of money on a designated rooftop by four o'clock that afternoon. Gertrude's assignment was to pose as the daughter and place the money on the roof.

"I was scared out of my wits," she recalls, "but you don't let on that you're scared. The detectives assured me they would be covering the area and I would be protected. I had five flights of stairs to climb to get to the top. All the way up I kept hearing noises and I'd think, 'Oh God! What's that?' Each time they turned out to be harmless. Then I kept thinking, 'Can I really do it?' When I reached the roof I put the envelope where I had been told to put it and nothing happened. Downstairs the detectives said I was finished with the job and I should go back to the academy. Going back uptown, I really felt great. All the way on the subway I said to myself, 'Well, you did it and here you are in one piece.'"

After three months at the police academy Gertrude was awarded the trophy for general excellence and was assigned with all the other women to the Bureau of Policewomen. Later she was assigned to the Youth Aid Division, where she worked with young people who had been picked up but were not being arrested. "In effect, I was a case investigator," she explains. "I would try to do something to help the kids who were in trouble but who weren't really serious offenders."

In addition to her work with children, Gertrude was receiving special assignments. One was to get into a private gambling club, the 201 Club, and find out if it was operating illegally. Word had been received by Mayor Fiorello La Guardia of New York that the 201 Club was running illegal gin rummy and poker games. Gertrude remembers being called into the office of Deputy Chief Inspector Murphy along with another policewoman.

"He was an old-school Irish cop," she says, "and he spoke with a thick Irish brogue. He looked at us and said, 'Now listen. I want you two to get in there. I don't care how you do it and how long it takes, but you two better get in there. You're on your own.' So we walk out of there wondering. I mean what could we do? We couldn't get in there without a referral."

Fortunately they found someone to refer them. The other policewoman knew a man who ran a legitimate bridge club. He was a young single fellow, and when the two women came to his club on the pretext of wanting to play bridge (but really hoping to get a referral to the 201 Club), he was delighted. He called a friend of his and the two men took the women out for the evening.

"He didn't know we worked for the Police Department," Gertrude relates. "When he met my friend before, she had been working for the Department of Welfare, and he thought she was still there. We didn't tell them any different."

On the way home from the date the other policewoman innocently mentioned that she and Gertrude would love to play gin rummy at the 201 Club but they didn't know anyone who could get them in there.

"Oh, it's run by a friend of mine," said the bridge club owner. "Just use my name."

The next day the two women went to the 201 Club, used his name, and were admitted. They went back for several days, and before the week was out, they were able to ascertain that the club was operating illegally. The police raided the place and the owners were arrested and later tried.

"I felt terrible," confides Gertrude. "Actually, they were very nice people, and I had to point out who was doing what. Then, the people realized who sent us and they were furious with the man who ran the bridge club. I kept telling them he had nothing to do with it, but I don't think they believed me. It was fun working out the case and testifying in court—I turned out to be a very good testifier—but we felt like heels because we had deceived the innocent bridge club owner."

As a result of her work on the case of the 201 Club, Gertrude became a favorite with Deputy Chief Inspector Murphy, and whenever a woman was needed for special investigations, he requested her.

In January 1949, the Schimmels' first son, Victor, was born. Gertrude requested a leave of absence from the department and was granted six months. Later she was given a three month extension. "I always felt bad about that," she says. "I would have liked more time."

When she returned to work, Gertrude found that combining a career with motherhood presented problems. "It's very difficult," she relates. "You're smitten with guilt. It was terrible. I did all kinds of handstands in order to work and bring up my child. I got part-time help, which wasn't too satisfactory. But between my husband and myself, we kind of managed."

In October 1952, when the second son, Edward, was born, Gertrude boldly asked for a two year leave and, to her amazement, got it. She claims she was never bored during her time away from the Police Department. "It wasn't as though I was going to stay home forever," she explains. "I knew I had a job to go back to."

At the end of two years Gertrude felt she wanted to be more than a part-time mother. She also wanted to continue as a policewoman. The solution was to work nights—a special double tour from 4:00 P.M. to 8:00 A.M.—on the youth escort car.

"The hours were long," Gertrude recalls, "but you only worked every third night. The hardest part was working twenty-four hours every third Sunday."

At first, sleeping during the day was difficult because Gertrude didn't have any help with the children. Eventually she found someone who could fit into her schedule, and she was able to get adequate rest. It was so successful that her children were hardly aware that she worked. Gertrude remembers a day when her older boy came home from kindergarten. He told her that the teacher had asked how many of the children's mothers worked and that a couple of kids had raised their hands. "What did you do?" his mother asked him. "I didn't raise my hand," he answered. "Well, why not?" she persisted. "Oh, you only work part-time," was his reply. Gertrude smiles when she tells the story. "It made me feel good that he didn't think of me as a working mother."

Gertrude was on the night shift for eight years. During that time her job involved servicing children who needed to be taken to a shelter in the middle of the night.

"I always considered that an important assignment," she says, "even though it looked like nothing—you know, ferrying kids. A lot of them are young kids whose mothers suddenly have to go to the hospital, and they're scared. They're pulled out of their beds and taken to the shelter. You have to have some kind of sensitivity with them. You have to be understanding with the girls who have been arrested and are being sent to Youth House.

"You might have someone doing the job who would just consider herself a chauffeur, but I tried, during the time the kids were with me, to prepare them or, in some cases, to make them a little less angry."

Gertrude recalls coming to pick up a fifteen-year-old girl who had been arrested. Apparently she and the arresting detective had had a row. The girl's dress was torn and she was in handcuffs.

"They usually don't handcuff juveniles," Gertrude explains, "but I guess that must have been some little fracas there. The detective said to me, 'You better not take her out of handcuffs. She's a wild one.' I asked her if she'd behave if I took off the handcuffs, but she was too angry to reply. So we go down to the car. We put her in the back of the station wagon and she's got the handcuffs on. It's going to be a long ride sitting in the back with handcuffs. So after we've gone about three or four blocks, I tell the driver to pull over to the curb. Now I turn around to the girl and I say, 'Look. I don't know what happened before we got there. Whatever you and the detective had, we're innocent of. It can't be very comfortable for you to sit there with handcuffs on. I'm willing to take them off if you behave.' She sort of grudgingly said okay and I took off the handcuffs, but she still wasn't too friendly. Then, as we drove along we started talking, and by the time we got to Youth House, we had things straightened out with the girl.

"That's what I mean by using that time to the best advantage. You're doing the most you can with her in a police situation, and maybe you're leaving her with a good taste for having met some understanding cops."

In 1958 Gertrude began work on a book for children called *Joan Palmer, Policewoman*. The heroine, Joan, was very much like the author, and her adventures were taken from the real-life career of Gertrude Schimmel. The book was published in 1960.

That same year Gertrude retired from the police force. The department offers a minimum twenty-year retirement policy, and having served that amount of time, the forty-one-year-old policewoman decided to quit in order to devote her energies to writing. Within two weeks after retiring, she knew she had made a mistake. When she applied to the police commissioner for reinstatement, she was informed that it was against department policy to reinstate retired persons.

Not one to give up easily, Gertrude started doing research on civil service laws. Feeling she had a good case for reinstatement, she hired a lawyer and went to court. "I happened to be the perfect person to break the policy," she explains. "Here I was, retired at the age of forty-one. That's very young to retire. Then, I had a wonderful record on the force, and I had written a book, and I had all sorts of recommendations. Anyway, we went into court and won it."

Gertrude was no sooner back in the department when she became aware that her fight for reinstatement had sparked the beginnings of an even more important battle, the fight for promotion for women.

All through the years the New York City policewomen had the same rights as the policemen—except one. They were excluded from regular civil service promotion to the ranks of sergeant, lieutenant, and captain.

Impressed by Gertrude's successful lawsuit, another policewoman, Felicia Schpritzer, decided that she and Gertrude could go to court and win the right to promotion for the women of the Police Department. Since promotion was achieved by passing an examination, Felicia, knowing she would be turned down, applied to take the exam for sergeant. She was refused. "Then," recalls Gertrude, "she prepared to go to court to contest the refusal. We could tell we had a good case. Felicia knew where to dig out certain things from the city charter. We amassed the facts. It was a beautiful case and we knew we couldn't lose it. We were prepared to go as high as the United States Supreme Court.

"Of course," she continues, "in the beginning people kept

saying it wouldn't work, that men won't respect women bosses and that there'll be all kinds of fights. Felicia used to go around arguing with these people. I'd say, 'Save your breath. What they say doesn't matter. If we win in court and they have to give us an exam and we become promoted, it's a fait accompli. They're stuck with us. Once that happens, they'll accept it.' "

As the two women had predicted, they won their case in court, and as Gertrude had foreseen, once it was department policy, everyone accepted it.

On March 13, 1965, the *New York Post* printed a news item with the headline, "SCHPRITZER AND SCHIMMEL BECOME THE FIRST FEMALE SERGEANTS IN THE DEPARTMENT'S HISTORY." The report went on to say, "Two motherly looking matrons wearing .32 caliber Smith & Wesson revolvers on their hips opened new horizons for the aspiring policewoman yesterday by achieving the rank of sergeant in the New York City Police Department."

Once promotion was open to women, Gertrude vowed she would not stop until she achieved the highest civil service rank of captain. In December of 1967, Gertrude Schimmel and Felicia Schpritzer became the first female lieutenants in the department, and in August 1971, Gertrude Schimmel, fifty-two, was sworn in as the first woman captain (Felicia came out lower on the list and has not yet been reached for appointment). A picture in the *New York Times* shows Gertrude flashing a radiant smile. Her comment upon achieving captaincy was, "We liberated the Police Department." In the same interview she added, "I have no problem being a boss to men. When you're boss, that's that. . . ."

As captain, she was placed in charge of the Policewomen's Section and became instrumental in helping to lay the groundwork for an experiment with policewomen on patrol.

In January 1972, Captain Schimmel was appointed deputy inspector and named commanding officer of the Youth Aid Division. Then, in April 1974, after heading the Police Commissioner's Editorial Review Board, she was made commanding officer of the Public Information Division. On November 1, 1974, she became a full inspector— the highest-ranking woman on the force.

The office of Inspector Gertrude Schimmel is as unpretentious as the woman who inhabits it. Standard black filing cabinets line one-half of a wall, and the simple desk features a telephone, assorted papers, and a pen set on a marble base with the inscription, "CAPTAIN GERTRUDE D. T. SCHIMMEL. FIRST LADY CAPTAIN."

On a July afternoon Inspector Schimmel is dressed in her standard summer attire—a shirtwaist dress. "A shirtwaist," she reveals, "makes it easier to get at my gun, which I wear underneath the dress." She explains that it is simpler to choose a winter wardrobe. "Then I can wear the gun under a coat."

Today Inspector Schimmel says she is tired, having been up late the night before. To an observer she appears incredibly lively. She is involved in endless phone conversations— all in a day's work—and each call is taken with great spirit. She listens attentively, interspersing her listening with dozens of "yeahs" and bursts of energetic laughter. Between phone calls, forms and letters are brought for the inspector to sign. Then Gertrude puts on horn-rimmed glasses and reads the designated paper carefully before affixing her signature to it.

During the occasional interruptions from office activity, Gertrude speaks avidly about her philosophy as a policewoman, her feelings concerning her future, and the experiment with women on patrol.

"I feel as though I've had two careers. For the first

Gertrude Schimmel

twenty-four years I was a policewoman. Then from 1965 to the present, I've had a career as an officer. Now I'm an administrator, and I work directly under the deputy commissioner of public information. We give information to the press. We get all sorts of requests for information from all parts of the country as well as the city. We also get requests for speakers. We publish the department magazine and the police commissioner's newsletter. We write the police commissioner's speeches. We issue press cards. I like it. I'm at the heart of everything. I know what's going on all over the department.

"I have very strong feelings about ethics in the Police Department and always have had. I remember when I was in my twenties and working in Juvenile Aid, a grateful mother sent me a ten-dollar gift certificate. A sergeant advised me to keep it and I was horrified. I wouldn't even accept a cup of coffee and he was telling me to take a ten dollar gift certificate. I've always felt it was demeaning to take anything. The practice in the past was that a cop would be out patroling and would step into a coffee shop and be given a cup of coffee. I never could do that. A lot of people say, 'What's a cup of coffee?' I say a cup of coffee is a lot. It can lead to other things. Why should a storekeeper give you a cup of coffee? Then he should give it to the postman, the sanitation guy, and everyone else. Soon he'll be working for nothing. Sometimes a policewoman will say that you hurt the merchant's feelings by refusing the coffee or whatever is offered. I don't buy that. When you make it clear that you don't take gifts, they'll accept that.

"I'm in favor of women on patrol. Even though a lot of people object to the idea, it will gradually become accepted. There's the notion that patroling is a man's job. The truth is, only a very small percentage of calls require physical force. Of the police calls that come in, 80 to 90 percent are service jobs—handling accidents, settling disputes, and giving information. It's one of the myths of police work that you need a lot of physical force. You have an image of a big, brawny cop striding down the street. It really isn't that kind of work. Even the situations that require some force may not have needed it if the cop had handled the situation differently. There have been cases that have shown that women can handle these potentially violent situations somewhat better than men. Women, by their conditioning, use more tact and persuasion. They just don't start out being aggressive in a way that evokes counteraggression.

"The question is, how much strength does a woman need to patrol? Policewomen are healthy specimens to begin with, and they are well-trained. You are rarely, if ever, alone. Women in the experiments successfully handled the psycho situations, which are really the most dangerous. Women have helped carry heavy people down several flights of stairs. In the one-year experiment women did just about all the things they would be called on to do in various situations. If the woman can do the work and wants to do the work, she should be allowed to do it, even if the men have feelings against it.

"The Police Department has a mandatory retirement age of sixty-three, which means I could stay eight more years. I'm not sure I'll stay the full eight years. I've been on the force for a long time—longer than most. I even have seniority over the police commissioner. Once I retire, I don't think I'll take up a new career. If I do anything at all it will be some kind of writing on my own."

It's 5:00 P.M., and Inspector Gertrude Schimmel, who earlier claimed fatigue, is still talking briskly on the phone and discussing problems with reporters and police personnel who come into her office. Her voice is clear and sharp, and her warm laugh erupts as readily as it did five hours ago.

It would be interesting to see her on a day when she is not tired.

Gloria Steinem

Gloria Steinem has the flu. Her head aches, her throat is raw, and her eyes are watery and heavy-lidded. Her temperature is 102 degrees. She has just finished a day of work at *Ms.* magazine, which she cofounded and where she is an editor, but instead of rushing home, she is zipping up her fleece-lined suede coat, preparing to go to Westport, Connecticut, where she is scheduled to make two speeches.

The car that takes her to Westport is tiny, and Gloria is wedged uncomfortably in the backseat between two reporters who are writing stories about her and *Ms.* During the hour-and-a-half ride she generously answers any questions the journalists ask her, politely turning from side to side as she gives them both her full attention.

There will be no time to eat supper between speaking engagements, but Gloria doesn't complain. She accepts the situation just as she accepts the bumper-to-bumper traffic out of New York and the cramped conditions in the car.

The first stop in Westport is at a large, beautiful home. Inside a capacity crowd is having a fund-raising wine and cheese party for the Connecticut Woman's Caucus. Gloria is the guest of honor. As she starts toward the brightly lit house, Gloria turns to one of the reporters and says wistfully, "Oh, let's all go home. Wouldn't it be nice to be watching a movie on TV?" Then she laughs, pulls up her coat collar, tucks her hands into her pockets, and continues up the drive.

When she enters the party, a voice calls out, "Here's our star." Gloria flinches at the word *star* but says nothing. Everyone is staring at her, comparing her real-life self to her photographs and her television appearances. "She looks different," observes one young woman.

Gloria takes off her coat. She is wearing a pair of corduroy pants and a print shirt over a pink turtleneck—the same clothes she has had on since nine o'clock in the morning. Her face is without makeup, and her thick straight brown hair hangs below her shoulders. Her only adornment is a large pair of purple-rimmed glasses.

People shake Gloria's hand, crowd around her, and ask her questions or remind her of other meetings they have both attended. Her response to everyone is warm and friendly. She is pulled over to the fireplace, where she will stand and speak. But first the introductions. As Gloria waits to be introduced, she appears to be falling asleep with weariness. The lids of her eyes grow heavy, and it's only with effort that she manages to keep them from closing.

Then she is on. She stands informally before the large assemblage, wide awake now. Her talk is brief. She emphasizes that women must try to get away from stereotypes and view each other as individuals. "Sometimes we need to exclude men from our organizations in order for women to learn to work together," she says. "We need our own psychic turf."

A half hour later, as she leaves the party, she is told that one of the male guests has commented on her tremendous poise and assurance. "He should only know," she replies laughing. Then she adds, "It sure beats writing."

Her second enormous audience, at the Westport Playhouse, is composed of men and women of all ages. The occasion is a fund-raising drive for the feminist newsletter

(*Photo by Chie Nishio*)

Alert. Gloria asks for the houselights so she can see the people. She makes many points during her hour talk, relating political issues to everyday life. For instance: The women's movement is prowoman and not antimale; parents should share responsibility for children. "Let's have parenthood," she urges, "not just motherhood." She asserts that women must be paid more money—the difference between male and female pay has gotten worse; that housework is respectable—that's why men should share in it; and that women should not be afraid of acting unfeminine—aggressive, loud, or strong—to get what they are entitled to.

The lively question and discussion period after her talk is the part Gloria likes best. She becomes so involved in the interaction that she forgets she is sick.

The drive back to New York starts at 10:45. Gloria is interviewed by one of the reporters during the trip, and as she answers the questions her sore throat begins to sound hoarse.

At midnight a feverish and exhausted Gloria climbs into bed. Except for having the flu, it has been a fairly typical day for one of the most important figures of the women's movement.

Making the best of difficult situations is nothing new for Gloria Steinem. Her early years were an invaluable (though not necessarily desirable) training period for her present adaptability. From the day of her birth in Toledo, Ohio, on March 25, 1934, to her eleventh year, Gloria's life was predominantly nomadic. Summers were spent in a resort in Michigan owned by her father. In the winter the family— Gloria, her mother and father, and her older sister Suzanne—piled into a trailer and headed for Florida or California. They would travel about, living in the trailer while Mr. Steinem earned money buying and selling antiques.

"My mother would have liked a more stable life," Gloria

recalls, "to stay home and to have a regular house. But not my father. He loved travel and change and uncertainty. He never put a real bathroom or real heating in our summer place because he was afraid we'd insist on staying home during the winter."

Despite the fact that she sometimes wanted to go to school and live a life more like that of the children she read about or saw in movies, Gloria claims she never resented her father. "It's true he wasn't a responsible person in the conventional sense," she says warmly, "but he couldn't help being the way he was. He always had dreams that great things were going to happen the next day or the next. I worry that just before he died he had to face the fact that nothing very spectacular was going to happen after all."

The Steinems were divorced when Gloria was eleven. Her sister, ten years older than Gloria, had finished school and was working. Gloria and her mother moved to the industrial slums of east Toledo. Although a house was given to them by Mrs. Steinem's family, they were poorer than the others in the neighborhood who worked in factories. Mrs. Steinem wasn't working and their only income was from renting a part of the house. "To tell you the truth," says Gloria, "I don't know how we managed to get along. But we did—just barely."

Reading books became a bright activity in her drab life. She would go to the local library, start at the top shelf of a row of books, and indiscriminately read her way down. She doesn't remember any of her school friends sharing her addiction to reading. They considered it a craziness on Gloria's part. Real life to the factory workers' children of east Toledo was going to the movies, basketball games, Hungarian festivals, and Polish weddings. "They were having a good time," Gloria comments, "for the few years until they would have to work in factories too."

In high school Gloria began to dream of an escape from

the acute poverty of her home life. She fantasized getting married at the age of sixteen or seventeen to someone who worked in a factory. She would take care of a clean little house and have babies. Her other dream was to become a dancer. She had been dancing for the Eagles (a group similar to the Elks) on Saturday nights, making ten dollars for two shows.

"I wanted to be a dancer," she recalls, "because the only women who looked as if they were leading exciting lives were in show business. I dreamed about that as an escape in much the same way that poor boys dream about becoming professional athletes." Ultimately it was her mother who provided an eternally grateful Gloria with a way out. She sold their house and used part of the money to send her daughter to college.

Gloria went to Smith, a small prestigious girls' college, the same school where her sister had gone ten years earlier when the family was together and in slightly better financial circumstances. "College changed my life," she reports. "They actually *wanted* you to read books. It was the first time I had met adults who liked books and cared about ideas."

In order to supplement the money she received from her mother, Gloria got scholarships and loans, worked in the summer, and waited tables during the school year.

After graduating magna cum laude, Gloria received a $1,000 Chester Bowles fellowship to go to India. "It was a sort of early peace corps," she explains. "Another girl and I were the first to go, so my project was to make a guide for future fellowship holders."

If Smith affected Gloria intellectually, India opened her eyes politically. She came to the country believing that had the Americans been the colonial power in India, they would have done better than the British. "I thought," relates Gloria, "that we would have been more democratic and encouraged self-rule, that we would have intermarried and disappeared. What I saw was that the Americans in India were as exploitative as the British. They were living in isolated wealth surrounded by the incredible poverty of the Indians. Then, too, Indians I met challenged my ideas of my own country. They asked me about the Civil War. I had always believed that the north had gone to war on the moral issue of slavery. My Indian friends made me aware that the south, with its slaves, was a threat to the newly in-dustrialized north and that the root of the war was at least partly economic, not moral."

When Gloria returned to the United States she felt she must alert other Americans to the world of poverty and in-justice she had discovered. "I wanted people here to know that the United States couldn't last," she says, smiling at her former naïvete. "I had an image of the United States as a big cupcake in the middle of people starving to death. I was sure all the other countries would turn on the United States and try to overthrow it. How could such abundance and such poverty continue to exist side by side?"

So deep was her sense of urgency that she went to foundations and to all the television networks trying to start some project that would teach people about South Asia and encourage this government toward more economic aid. Nobody was interested. "They were not only uninterested," observes Gloria dryly, "they were hostile or bored or amused."

Failing with the media, Gloria went to Cambridge in 1959 to work with a small group of internationally con-cerned students and young people who were urging people to go to the Communist Youth Festivals—frequently with no success. "My idea," she recalls, "was that we should reach out to other students across national boundaries. All most people I talked to cared about was whether or not they could ever get security clearance after attending a Communist-sponsored youth festival—and of course the predict-able answer in the 1950s was *no*."

In 1960 Gloria settled in New York and began to look for a job where she could use her political concern. Wherever she went, she was told she was overqualified for lower-level jobs and underqualified for top-level jobs. It was a period of terrible frustration. She thought about writing, but everyone told her that making a living as a writer was impossible, especially if you were a woman.

Marriage was something she assumed she would do, but in the future. "The idea of getting married right then terrified me," Gloria remembers. "It seemed my life would be over; my final choice made. I would think, 'Two years from now it would be terrific to get married, but not *now*.'"

In 1961 Gloria became part of a staff of three on a political satire magazine called *Help!* It was a part-time job and didn't pay much, but she learned a lot about how to put a magazine together. She also began doing some unsigned free-lance writing for *Esquire* magazine on such nonpolitical subjects as how to cook without really cooking and where to take girls on dates in New York City.

Her confidence in her writing ability was increasing, but her assignments continued to be frivolous. Says Gloria, "Women weren't supposed to know how to write on serious subjects." One of her most famous assignments was an article she did for *Show* magazine on being a Playboy bunny. Unknown to the Playboy Club, Gloria took the job in order to write about it. Her diary, describing her work as a bunny, was a wonderfully funny exposé of a totally unglamorous, exploited way of life.

"After doing that piece," recounts Gloria with a grimace, "I was even more typecast as a 'girl writer.' Editors would ask me to pose as a prostitute or commit myself to a mental institution in order to write about the experience. At parties

I'd be introduced as Gloria Steinem, a Playboy bunny, as if that had been my real job in life."

Most of her writing for the next five years consisted of profiles of movie stars, writers, and "beautiful people" of the society world. Even though she was sharing a one-room apartment with another girl and making very little money, it was assumed that her personal life resembled the world she wrote about. Because she went out with several well-known men and attended some big New York parties, she was thought to be a "beautiful person" herself. Her name and picture appeared in the newspapers and magazines, often the same ones that had refused her the political assignments they gave to less-experienced men writers.

In 1968 Clay Felker, the publisher of *New York* magazine, gave Gloria her first chance to be a political writer. She became a contributor to the magazine's weekly column "The City Politic" (the name was Gloria's idea). In addition to this regular feature on New York politics, she did an article on the 1968 presidential elections which included a famous interview with Patricia Nixon (as a woman reporter, Nixon's staff would not give her an interview with the candidate himself), an account of Nelson Rockefeller's trip to Latin American, and several articles against the war in Vietnam.

Shedding the social butterfly image that had built up around her, Gloria became increasingly involved with political causes. She worked for Cesar Chavez's migrant workers, for Eugene McCarthy, Robert Kennedy, Shirley Chisholm, and George McGovern. When she covered a meeting of Redstockings, a New York feminist group, and heard women talk honestly and publicly about their humiliating and dangerous experiences with abortion, she realized why she had been so consistently attracted to the causes of powerless groups. Women were discriminated against, too. For the first time she began to see women as a political group.

"I had always thought," she relates, "that prejudice against me as a woman was a personal problem—perhaps even my own fault. At that point I began to understand it was a group problem." It was the beginning of her role as an active feminist.

So deep was Gloria's commitment to the women's movement that despite the fact that getting up in front of an audience terrified her, she began to speak about feminism in public—the only way of getting the information out, she felt, since newspapers and magazines were largely disinterested. From 1969 to 1973 she talked to women in every section of the United States. She rarely spoke alone, usually sharing the podium with a black woman, often day care innovator Dorothy Pitman Hughes. "It made me feel more secure to be with someone else," Gloria confides. "I also thought it was good for political reasons. I didn't want to give the impression that the only women in the movement were white and college educated like myself. More important, we could both talk about the parallels between sexism and racism."

What thrilled her was that when she talked to women and exchanged experiences with them, class and economic differences lessened or melted away. In a meeting with a group of trade-union women in Chicago, Gloria had been hesitant to speak because the women might resent her. She decided to be present simply as a participant. After sitting through a day-long discussion, she was asked by the women if she would get up and talk. "Then we began to realize the same old thing," recounts Gloria. "The boundaries between us were not so great. As women, living in a patriarchy, we all share many of the same problems. The meeting ended up with all of us being terribly moved, many of us with tears in our eyes."

In Alabama Gloria, Dorothy, and another black woman, Margaret Sloan, were speaking to some black household workers who were organizing for better pay. There were also a few white women present. The white women asked Gloria about consciousness-raising or "rap" groups. "I explained to them," says Gloria, "that unlike men, who generally have a place to get together and talk, women really have no common meeting ground. We're very isolated from each other in our houses, taking care of our families, thinking that we're crazy, that there's something wrong with us if we're not fulfilled by the traditional subservient role. As I was talking about our aloneness, one of the white women began to cry. The black women, seeing a white woman cry, suddenly made a connection with her aloneness, her powerlessness. It was moving to see how black and white southern women could identify with each other. That group of women has stayed together to this day."

When Gloria was approached in 1970 about starting a feminist magazine, she reluctantly agreed to participate. "I didn't want to start a magazine or work on one," she explains. "I wanted to be a writer." Her agreement to work was based on the hope that it would be a means of raising money for an educational foundation she had helped to found, the Woman's Action Alliance, a nonprofit group that assisted women in their efforts to organize. Once she and the other editors began to think about the composition of a new magazine, the project took on a life of its own. Recalls Gloria, "It became a whole way of reaching out—a place for women to say what they had never been able to say in any other publication. Instead of how to make 101 kinds of hamburger, as in other women's magazines, we wanted to share and explore ways of changing our lives."

Gloria's role was to coordinate activities, write up article ideas, help make up a dummy, and look for possible investors. In the beginning, raising money seemed impossible. Other magazines were folding and here were these women asking men to give them money to start a new publication. Some companies were interested, but they made it clear that they didn't trust women to run the financial side. They would give funding if they could have control of the magazine. The women declined the offers.

Toward the end of 1971, Clay Felker, of *New York* magazine, decided he wanted something different for his year-end issue. He conceived of a sample section that would fit into the center of *New York*, and then with more material added to it, be distributed nationally as a separate magazine. He told Gloria and the other editors that he would finance a national sample issue for them if they would produce it first for him as an insert and share equally whatever profits there were with *New York*. He would not, however, demand any permanent share if the magazine continued.

The women were delighted. Here was a way of testing out their ideas on a nationwide scale. "We had this feeling," remembers Gloria, "that the first issue would be the last, so we kept working on it, trying to put in everything we wanted to say. There we were, all crammed into a little one-room office, working like crazy without salaries, hoping to make this thing perfect. Of course that was impossible, but we did try to include articles that would speak to women in many different situations."

The year-end issue of *New York* magazine, with the *Ms.* insert, was an enormous success. It sold better than any previous issue. Then the national issue came out on its own. There was little money for promotion, so all the writers and editors went around the country trying to get themselves on radio and television shows. They wanted women in other parts of the country to know about *Ms.*

"We had visions," says Gloria, "of our magazine just lying there on the newsstands, since we had no way of letting people know the issue was out. In San Francisco I was on a television program talking about *Ms.* Lots of people began to call in and ask, 'Where *is* this magazine?' I thought, 'Oh God! It never got here.' I called up Clay and said, 'Clay, it's not here. What's happened?' What had happened was that it had sold out. It had been designed to stay on the newsstand for two months, and it had sold out in a few days. We had been worn down by all the professionals telling us: 'It's too difficult'; 'People only watch television, they don't read magazines'; 'There aren't that many women who care about the women's movement.' But the professionals were wrong. The magazine was a success."

Gloria's desk in the *Ms.* office is in the corner of a large room that she shares with seven other editors. The office has a look of colorful disarray and features splashes of red, blue, and yellow in desk tops and camp chairs. There are touches of greenery at some desks, while others sport photographs and children's drawings.

The *Ms.* headquarters are as much a home to Gloria as her two-room East Side apartment—perhaps moreso, since she has come to regard the people at the magazine almost as her family.

In the 8:30 A.M. quiet of the *Ms.* office, Gloria, dressed in corduroy pants and a turtleneck sweater, sits at her slightly cluttered desk. Although it's the day after Thanksgiving and the office is officially closed, she has come in to "catch up on a few things." With slow, early-morning movements she sips from a container of coffee and talks about some of her ideas and goals.

"As a free-lance writer I almost always worked alone.

This is the first time that I've ever been involved in a communal enterprise, at least for more than a few months. There's a great satisfaction to it. I never had taken control of my life before. I was afraid to. I was convinced you were supposed to let outside forces take control, whether it was men you were going to marry or writing assignments or anything else. Now that I've made a commitment to the magazine, I could be quite happy working here for the rest of my life.

"My sister is married with six children. Her family is beginning to grow up and leave her. She is now finding other work to give meaning to her life. In my work there is progress and change; more than enough to last all my life.

"I enjoyed speaking around the country. Four years of that made me realize that the women's movement is the biggest and deepest and most important movement in the country. But I'm glad I don't have to speak so much anymore. In the beginning, when I was so terrified of making speeches, I would fortify myself by incredible research. I would dredge up all the facts I could find. I tried to speak extemporaneously with a lot of notes, although if it was a really important occasion I would get frightened enough to write it out word for word. At least you learn that when you have to make a speech you don't die. It was a fear I was glad to conquer. I can't say the fear never comes back. It's a little like malaria: You never totally get rid of it.

"I could never get married under the existing marriage laws, although I have been married every way except legally. The marriage laws are symbolic of what's wrong with the whole patriarchal system. A woman gives up her own name. Even her children will be identified by the man's name only. You lose a lot of your civil rights, your credit privileges, the right to establish your own legal residence, and many more. It's not so far from the old concept that the married couple is one person, and that person is the man.

"I think women or men who work in the home should be reimbursed. If a marriage is an equal partnership, then responsibilities and rewards must be equally shared. A wife who works at home is entitled to a legally determined percentage of her husband's salary. It should be hers and hers alone: After all, a widower would have to pay someone to take care of his house and children. She shouldn't have to ask for it, to beg for it, or feel guilty when she spends it. All human beings should have the freedom of having money that they have worked for and don't have to answer for.

"I doubt I will have children. There are children that I care about and are part of my life, but I don't think it matters very much whether they are my biological children or not. At one point I wanted to have children just so people wouldn't think I was crazy. Women who didn't have children were treated to a special kind of humiliation—they were called unfulfilled or even unnatural. But once you reject that idea, you begin to say, 'Children belong to all of us.'

"I'm still subject to plenty of the old female hangups, even in small ways. The other day I was standing on the curb with a man and we were looking for a taxi. He was looking in one direction and I was looking in another. I saw a taxi first and hailed it. It gave me a kind of odd feeling to be standing with a man and hailing a cab myself. If I were really free, I wouldn't even think about it. I would do what was most convenient and supportive of the other person.

"The most exciting part of my work is to see individual people change. The greatest satisfaction is to feel you are changing the world around you—but we are constantly plagued with doubt that we can really fundamentally change the power system based on sex and race. When I'm really depressed, I think that people in movements for social justice are living off the garbage heap of society, and because it's a rich society, it gets a rich garbage heap. We are tolerated up to the point of basic change, of changing who makes the garbage. But then we are in danger of being put down, not to rise again until another century."

It's 11:00 A.M. when Gloria finishes talking. She throws away the paper coffee container, clears her desk, and prepares for another long day of doing the work she loves.

Marcia Storch

Obstetrician–gynecologist Marcia Storch opened her practice in New York City in August 1973 with just a handful of patients. Then the word went around: Here at last was a doctor women could talk to, could ask questions of, and get respectful answers from; a doctor adolescent girls were able to feel comfortable with and one who would advise them honestly about sex and contraception. Six months later, in February 1974, she had 800 patients, and the list was still growing.

In the United States, according to the 1974 statistics, 97 percent of the obstetrician–gynecologists are men. Most women have always gone to male doctors to have their babies delivered, to discuss menstrual difficulties, to have vaginal examinations, and for birth control advice. Often they have been treated as stupid when they have asked questions about their own bodies. Sometimes they have been given medication and contraception without explanations of side effects, and many women recall unpleasant deliveries of their babies due to unsympathetic male obstetricians.

It is no wonder, then, that the pleasant waiting room of intelligent and compassionate Dr. Marcia Storch is continually crowded. Patients of all ages cheerfully wait as long as two hours for their appointments. As one eighteen year old says, "I don't mind waiting. I know when it's my turn I'll get my fair share."

A woman in her thirties adds, "There's a wonderful spirit in this office. Sometimes, if I'm in a hurry, another woman will let me go ahead of her, and I would do the same for someone else. I've never seen that happen in any other office."

"I went to my last gynecologist to discuss birth control," relates a twenty year old. "He said to me, 'Take the pill.' When I asked him if there were dangers or side effects, he said, 'Listen, I don't have time to explain everything. Either take it or don't take it. Here's a prescription.' Dr. Storch always has the time to explain," the young woman concludes with a smile.

As a young girl, Marcia Storch had no idea that she would grow up to be a successful and innovative physician. In fact, her early years were devoted almost entirely to music.

She was born February 21, 1933, in Pittsburgh, Pennsylvania. Her father was a chemist for the Bureau of Mines and became internationally famous for developing a method of making gasoline from coal. Her mother was a housewife who always deferred to her husband. "It was many years," recalls Marcia, "before my mother would even go to a movie without my father."

A very musically talented child, Marcia gave her first concert on the piano when she was three and a half. At the age of ten she abandoned the piano in favor of the violin.

"I suspect if it hadn't been a sexist world," Marcia conjectures, "I would have been a composer and a conductor. I was very frustrated in that direction. I was told to practice hard so I would be a joy to my husband and my children. There was never any indication that I could have a career."

Her father would have liked her to become a chemist, but, as with music, his goals for her were limited. He

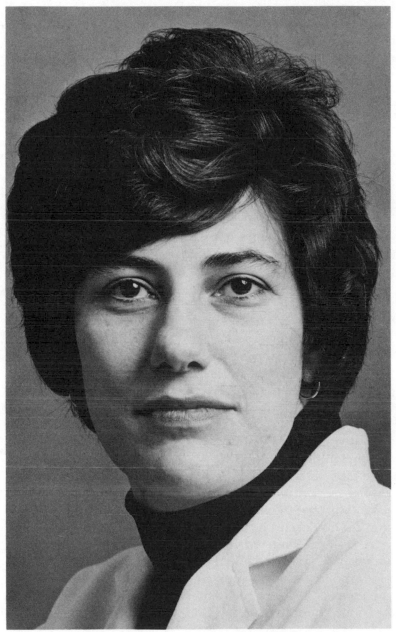

(*Photo by Eric Stephen Jacobs*)

expected her to get a bachelor's degree and then go to work in a drug company. "I don't think it occurred to my father," comments Marcia, "that I could ever do any original research. Perhaps because of his attitude, or maybe just out of simple rebellion, I never took any science courses in school."

An incident occurred when Marcia was two and a half which she claims to remember very clearly and which she thinks might have had an unconscious influence on her going into medicine many years later. Her five-year-old sister died due to a misdiagnosis by the family doctor.

When her sister became ill, Marcia's mother told the doctor that she thought her daughter had appendicitis. She said she preferred an unnecessary operation rather than taking a chance that the little girl die of a ruptured appendix. The doctor insisted that the child did not have appendicitis. Mrs. Storch then pleaded that he use the new sulfa drugs on her daughter. The doctor refused, saying they were still too experimental. The child died of a ruptured appendix.

If her sister's death didn't affect Marcia's choice of a career, it did instill in her the notion that often the patient can be right and the physician wrong—a concept that she still believes in.

Growing up in Pittsburgh did not provide a particularly happy childhood for Marcia. A tall, olive-skinned, dark-eyed girl, she was one of two Jewish children in a Christian community. She recalls that she was perfectly willing to assimilate "but the community was not willing to assimilate me. I was kicked and beaten and stoned for being Jewish during the Second World War. I was totally ostracized. I was never invited to birthday parties, and when I was older, no boys asked me on dates. Oh yes, there was one," she amends. "A very nice boy asked me on a Presbyterian hayride. My only date."

In high school Marcia gave up music and became intent on a writing career. Her essays and poetry constantly appeared in the school literary magazine, and she won an important prize for an essay on Edna St. Vincent Millay.

Her grades were always excellent. "I rarely studied," she recalls. "I could easily read, and still do, a thousand words a minute, so I just read everything." She now wonders if her dislike for studying might have been another factor in her avoidance of science courses. "There was a substitute teacher in high school," Marcia reports, "who suggested I would make a very good biologist, but I discounted biology because I knew it involved a lot of work."

When she finished high school, Marcia enrolled as a philosophy major at Bryn Mawr. Since her father was unwilling to pay for college, she obtained a partial scholarship. "My mother helped me out with savings from her household money," Marcia says, "but my father really believed that you shouldn't help children or they will turn out bad."

It was her studies in philosophy that led Marcia toward an interest in medicine. "I became fascinated by the philosophical distinction between what is real and what is abstract," she explains. "For example, if you sit on a table, does it make it a chair? You sit on it and it functions as a chair, yet it is still defined as a table. I was interested in how the mind separates these things, and that took me into the study of how the image that the eye sees is sent to the brain. I wondered how the brain stores the image and then puts it together with other data and eventually formulates it into language."

In her quest for answers, Marcia started studying social psychology. That led her into experimental psychology, which in turn fanned an interest in neurophysiology—the study of the workings of the nervous system.

Says Marcia, "In my junior year, when I became involved in neurophysiology, I began to realize that my real interest was in medicine. When I took biology in my senior year and liked it a lot and did very well in it, I knew I wanted to go to medical school."

In 1955, when she graduated from Bryn Mawr, Marcia's father made it clear that there would be no more money from home for her future education. "That was all right with me," Marcia comments. "I don't think I felt unhappy about it."

Then she began a series of jobs in an effort to save for her tuition. She washed test tubes in the microbiology laboratory at Harvard University for six months while taking science courses at night at Boston University. From there she took a teaching job and moved in with her parents, who were now living in Greenwich, Connecticut.

"I thought I would save money by living at home," she remembers. "It didn't work out that way. I was making $3,000 a year teaching high school while taking classes at night, but I was never able to save. My mother insisted I dress well, according to Greenwich standards, and my wardrobe expenses went way up. I had to maintain a car, since my job was thirty miles away, so that was another expense. At the end of two years I realized that maintaining a full-time job while taking classes was too much. Part-time positions weren't too plentiful in Connecticut, and I decided to move to New York."

During the period in Connecticut, Marcia remembers becoming engaged and unengaged several times. "I think any marriage I would have made would have been a disaster," she comments. "I realized at that time that I was a perfectionist and very demanding. I would have been difficult to live with. The men who wanted to marry me needed support and strength in their lives. I knew that I needed the same thing, and I wasn't about to become a helpmate to anyone else. My feeling was that the time to get married is when things are going well for two people individually, and not otherwise. Also, due to my upbringing, my expectations of people were unrealistically high and I wasn't a very sympathetic person."

At the age of twenty-five, in 1958, Marcia moved to New York. Her first job was to go through old newspapers to check on the number of times General Motors was mentioned in them. Two months later she was hired as a record librarian in steroid biochemistry by Columbia University College of Physicians and Surgeons. "The work was to take six months," says Marcia, "and I completed it in two months. They were so amazed and happy that they hired me fulltime as a laboratory technician." Of course, at night she was still making up science courses.

By December of 1958, Marcia decided that although she hadn't saved the requisite amount of money, it was time to apply to medical school. If accepted, she would take out a loan. She was accepted by Woman's Medical College in Philadelphia, and in September 1959, at the age of twenty-six, she began her studies to become a doctor.

"In those days Woman's Medical College was a terrible place," recalls Marcia. "Just awful. It was like going back to parochial school. We were told, 'Now girls, don't leave your coats in the hall.' " Marcia's pleasantly low voice goes into a mimicking falsetto. " 'Don't chew gum in class.' I couldn't believe it. Worst of all, the young women students sat there and took that kind of treatment. Some of the stuff that was being taught was thirty years out of date and it was wrong."

Marcia hastens to add that the medical school is now called the Medical College of Pennsylvania and has improved tremendously.

As a result of always being in conflict with her professors and because she questioned the quality of teaching, Marcia graduated from medical school in the lower fourth of her class. By contrast, she was awarded two prizes (only eight graduating prizes were given), the Professors' Prize in Psychiatry, and the Mosby Scholarship Award for Obstetrics.

Marcia's decision to specialize in obstetrics was arrived at during her internship. Due to a shortage of residents she was asked by the chief resident if she would like to deliver a baby. "The woman had been given a low spinal and was ready to deliver," remembers Marcia. "I said, 'Yes, I would like to do it.' I had delivered twelve or thirteen babies as a medical student, so I had some knowledge of what I was doing. After I scrubbed and examined the patient, the chief resident asked me what position the head was in. I told him and he didn't say anything. Then he asked me to describe the way the bones came together in the head. I did, and he still didn't say anything. 'Well, I guess I'm wrong,' I said to him. 'I guess it's the opposite way.' He said yes, I had gotten it wrong, but it wasn't that important and I should go ahead and apply the forceps to either side of the baby's head. I couldn't get the forceps to lock correctly. I tried about three times. Then he tried and couldn't get them to work either. I had been right, after all, about the position of the head, and he had been wrong. He turned the head around and I reapplied the forceps and delivered the baby. That was a big thrill. The joy of delivering the baby was such fun that I thought, 'Gee, if I like doing it so much, maybe that's what I ought to do.' I decided to specialize in obstetrics and gynecology."

During her residency Marcia began to formulate ideas that she would later employ in her own practice. One was that people be informed about their symptoms, shown the alternative treatments, and allowed to make their own decisions.

"Day in and day out," she remembers, "I would see male doctors telling their female patients what to do, with total disregard toward what the women wanted and with no real explanations of why they were using a certain treatment rather than another one. It bothered me a lot. The women were regarded as a sort of inferior species, as though they didn't have the intelligence, if given some alternatives, to decide what they wanted done to their bodies. I knew that when I started to practice I would tell my patients the facts and allow them to make decisions."

In the fall of 1967 Marcia completed her residency and was awarded a National Institute of Health Fellowship, which enabled her to spend the next two years studying and doing research in reproductive endocrinology. In 1969, instead of going into private practice, she entered the academic world as an assistant professor of obstetrics and gynecology at the University of Illinois. She also practiced and did research. Her next post was at Columbia University in New York City, where she was an assistant professor in obstetrics and gynecology and a research assistant in endocrinology at the International Institute for Human Reproduction.

At Columbia Marcia started to become aware of a sexual inequality in her field. "I began to realize," she recalls, "that the women were not paid or promoted equally with men. Even at places where women received equal pay, they still couldn't get equal work. Sure it's dandy if you're a female assistant professor and you're getting the same pay as a male assistant professor. But if you can't rise above the position of assistant professor, no matter how professionally competent you are, then it doesn't really matter.

"It's strange," muses Marcia. "I had no feminist consciousness when I decided to become an obstetrician. In fact, I had no awareness of any discrimination against women in medicine until 1969. At that time I was asked if I'd be interested in a staff position at a university and I said I would and why didn't they make me an offer? The man answered, 'Well, I'll have to ask the rest of the staff how they would feel about having a woman on staff.' I was taken aback. That was the first time I had heard anything like that."

In 1972 Marcia went to New York's Roosevelt Hospital as the only endocrinologist in the department of obstetrics and gynecology. It was agreed that she would divide her time between research, teaching, and seeing patients, including participation in an adolescent clinic. As it turned out, due to a cutback in funds, there was no research.

"There's little reason to be in the academic community if you're not doing research," observes Marcia, "and I felt I would be happier and better off in my own practice rather than in a group practice."

In August 1973 Marcia opened her office. The few patients she had been seeing at Roosevelt came with her. Women began to tell other women about the fine new doctor in town who actually took time with her patients, who listened to them, and who didn't make them feel like another body on a table. Feminist groups became interested in the intelligent, well-spoken young physician, and Marcia was besieged with speaking engagements, interviews, and consultations.

All the while, her practice continued to grow.

On a day when she has no office hours, Dr. Marcia Storch sits back in a leather chair in her air-conditioned office, calls her telephone answering service to let them know where she is, and quickly goes through the day's mail. She is dressed in simple pants and a shirt. Her newly short, thick brown hair accentuates her strong jaw and Slavic cheekbones.

With evident pleasure, she begins to talk about some of her theories on the practice of medicine.

"When I started my practice I made it a point to tell my

patients a great deal across the desk. Then I became aware
that patients were interested in learning about what was
going on in their own bodies, so I began to tell people what
I was doing while I was examining them. Now I teach every
patient to examine her own breasts. I show every patient,
who wants to see, her cervix and her vagina in the mirror. I
do a lot more explanations of the various infections than I
used to do. In a way, by helping patients understand and
find symptoms, you've gone one step toward preventive
medicine.

"I know some physicians might feel that by giving
patients so much information you are frightening them. I
happen to feel that people deal better with things they
understand. Occasionally I'll get a patient who will say,
'Look, I don't want to know anything about it. Just do what
you have to do and don't tell me anything.' I accept that in
the patient, but that patient is very rare—about one
percent of my practice.

"When I see adolescent girls, I will teach them about
anatomy—about the male and female reproductive system.
If they are there to learn about birth control, I'll go into the
various kinds of contraceptives available and I'll tell them
the hazards and advantages of each one. One thing I tell the
girls is that there is no rule about having or not having sex.
Today a lot of kids are under pressure to have sex when they
don't feel ready for it. They get the message that all the kids
are doing it and they should do it. On the other hand, there
are young people who have started a sexual relationship,
want to maintain it, and feel they must be clandestine because of their parents. I tell the girls that the decision about
sex is up to them—not to their peer group, not to their
parents.

"I have a number of people come to me with chronic, un-
resolved problems. These people with undiagnosed symptoms are usually women who have not been listened to by

their doctors. If the doctors had really listened, they would have gotten the diagnosis. I enjoy diagnostic problems." Marcia smiles, "I suspect for the same reason I enjoy mystery stories. I think that if a patient has a symptom you have to assume that the symptom is real until you can prove otherwise. Even then, I think there is some doubt."

With someone who is dying, Marcia feels the patient's questions should be answered. "Patients have very complex lives that include finances and dependents. I think it's extremely unfair to withhold information if there were things those people would do if they knew they were going to die. On the other hand, I don't believe one should force people to be realistic about something they don't want to be realistic about.

"I'm very neutral about the subject of natural childbirth. Some patients have had marvelous experiences with natural childbirth and some not so marvelous. My tendency is to support the patient in whatever her choice is. I don't think my patients who have natural childbirth are bigger and better than those who don't. Recently, one couple said they wanted to have me deliver their baby at their home. I was very hesitant. Not only would it take up a lot of my time, but if there's an emergency situation, you're really in trouble without all the hospital facilities. Finally I agreed to do it. The woman had natural childbirth and I stayed with her during labor. I got to the house around one o'clock in the afternoon and the baby was born at six. The husband was there and so were the two sets of grandparents-to-be. It turned out just great. The woman delivered in a chair and it was a wonderful experience for all of us. I wouldn't do it again, though, unless I had a team of nurse-midwives and a truck for emergencies.

"I'm finding that private practice, especially in places like New York City, is becoming increasingly difficult because of rising costs. My expenses are enormous. Then too, you can't do solo practice for very long without killing yourself. You're on call twenty-four hours a day if you're in obstetrics and gynecology. I have thirteen babies due within the next two months. The chances of my spending a weekend away from the city are negligible. I have to be able to get back very quickly. Of course I could have someone cover for me, but most of my patients expect to be delivered by me and are contracted to be delivered by me.

"If there were more women physicians around in my speciality I would take a partner, but I'm having trouble finding one. I would be willing to take a man as a partner, but I don't think my patients would accept a male doctor. You have to face the fact that most of the women who come into this office have been to six men and that's why they are here.

"I'm involved in the talking stages of an idea that could be an alternative to private practice. It would be the establishment of a professional women's center. We envision a funded service organization that would provide legal, mental health, social, and medical services for women. It might be an interesting solution and would involve community participation, which I think is good."

Marcia's final point is that she is always willing to admit to a patient that she is wrong or doesn't know something.

"I let my patients know that I'm not infallible, and they accept that." She continues to speak intensely and with great honesty. "In certain areas where my background is not very strong, I never hesitate to refer or ask for help. If there is any doubt in my mind, I'd rather call somebody and have them tell me I'm wrong or have them say, 'Gee, this is so obvious.' I'm a very compulsive person when it comes to medicine. Perhaps too much so. I would much rather look foolish or stupid than make an error that would harm a patient. A dumb question never killed anyone. It's that simple."

Suggested Reading

Auriol, Jacqueline, translated by Pamela Swinglehurst. *I Live to
Fly.* New York: Dutton, 1970. The world's only female test
pilot describes her comeback.

Bird, Caroline. *Born Female.* Rev. ed. New York: McKay, 1970.
The case for legal equality.

Bolton, Carole. *Never Jam Today.* New York: Atheneum, 1973
(paper). Maddy pickets the White House in 1917.

Chamberlin, Hope. *A Minority of Members: Women in the U.S.
Congress.* New York: New American Library, 1974 (paper).

Crary, Margaret. *Susette La Flesche: Voice of the Omaha
Indians.* New York: Hawthorn Books, 1973.

Dash, Joan. *A Life of One's Own: Three Gifted Women and the
Men They Married.* New York: Harper & Row, 1973.

DeMille, Agnes. *To A Young Dancer.* Boston: Little Brown.
Heartaches and big breaks in the world of dance, by the
noted dancer and choreographer.

Faber, Doris. *Petticoat Politics: How American Women Won the
Right to Vote.* New York: Lothrop, Lee & Shepard, 1967.

Fleming, Alice. *Great Women Teachers.* Philadelphia:
Lippincott, 1965. Ten pioneers in American education.

Gersh, Harry. *Women Who Made America Great.* Philadelphia:
Lippincott. Women in careers ranging from astronomy to
engineering.

Gerson, Noel B. *Daughter of Earth and Water: A Biography of
Mary Wollstonecraft Shelley.* New York: Morrow, 1973.

Greenfeld, Howard. *Gertrude Stein: A Biography.* New York:
Crown, 1973.

Gridley, Marion E. *American Indian Women.* New York:
Hawthorn Books, 1974.

Hershan, Stella K. *A Woman of Quality: Eleanor Roosevelt.* New
York: Crown.

Suggested Reading

Howe, Florence and Ellen Bass. *No More Masks: An Anthology of Poems by Women.* New York: Doubleday, 1973.

Kahn, Kathy. *Hillybilly Women.* New York: Doubleday, 1973. Mountain women speak of their struggle and joy in southern Appalachia.

Komisar, Lucy. *The New Feminism.* New York: Franklin Watts, 1971.

Lerner, Gerda (editor). *Black Women in White America.* New York: Pantheon, 1972.

Mead, Margaret. *Blackberry Winter: My Earlier Years.* New York: Morrow, 1972.

Meltzer, Milton. *Tongue of Flame: The Life of Lydia Maria Child.* New York: T. Y. Crowell, 1965. A biography of the unsung political writer and author of the first antislavery book published in America.

Merriam, Eve (editor). *Growing Up Female in America.* New York: Dell, 1973 (paper). Accounts of ten lives in different times and places.

Nathan, Dorothy. *Women of Courage.* New York: Random House, 1964. Profiles of Susan B. Anthony, Jane Addams, Mary Bethune, Amelia Earhart, Margaret Mead.

Noble, Iris. *Cameras and Courage: Margaret Bourke-White.* New York: Masner, 1973.

Petry, Ann. *Harriet Tubman: Conductor of the Underground Railroad.* New York: T. Y. Crowell, 1955.

Ross, Pat (editor). *Young and Female: Turning Points in the Lives of Eight American Women.* New York: Random House, 1972.

Schulman. L. M. (editor). *A Woman's Place: An Anthology of Short Stories.* New York: Macmillan, 1974. Ten contemporary short stories by women, about women.

Seed, Suzanne. *Saturday's Child.* Chicago: O'Hara, 1973. Accounts of women in thirty-six nontraditional careers.

Sterling, Philip. *Sea and Earth: The Life of Rachel Carson.* New York: T. Y. Crowell, 1970.

Teitz, Joyce. *What's a Nice Girl Like You Doing in a Place Like This?* New York: Coward McCann, 1972. Accounts of women in male-dominated professions.

Index

Index

Index

Index

174